communication @ work

H. NORMAN WRIGHT

Regal

A Division of Gospel Light
Ventura, California, U.S.A.

Published by Regal Books
A Division of Gospel Light
Ventura, California, U.S.A.
Printed in the U.S.A.

Regal Books is a ministry of Gospel Light, an evangelical Christian publisher dedicated to serving the local church. We believe God's vision for Gospel Light is to provide church leaders with biblical, user-friendly materials that will help them evangelize, disciple and minister to children, youth and families.

It is our prayer that this Regal book will help you discover biblical truth for your own life and help you meet the needs of others. May God richly bless you.

For a free catalog of resources from Regal Books/Gospel Light, please call your Christian supplier or contact us at 1-800-4-GOSPEL or www.regalbooks.com.

Cover and Interior Design by Robert Williams
Edited by Deena Davis

Library of Congress Cataloging-in-Publication Data
Wright, H. Norman.
    Communication @ work / H. Norman Wright.
       p. cm.
    Includes bibliographical references.
    ISBN 0-8307-2777-9
Communication in organizations. 2. Interpersonal relations. I. Title: Communication at work. II. Title.

HD30.3 .W75 2001
650.1'3—dc21
                                        2001019318

1 2 3 4 5 6 7 8 9 10 11 12 13 14 15 / 09 08 07 06 05 04 03 02 01

Rights for publishing this book in other languages are contracted by Gospel Literature International (GLINT). GLINT also provides technical help for the adaptation, translation and publishing of Bible study resources and books in scores of languages worldwide. For further information, contact GLINT, P.O. Box 4060, Ontario, CA 91761-1003, U.S.A. You may also send e-mail to Glintint@aol.com, or visit their website at www.glint.org.

CONTENTS

CHAPTER 1

IT'S ABOUT PEOPLE!

I really like my job. The work is fulfilling and challenging. I feel productive and it's a good organization to be with. The only problem is, well . . . although some of the people you end up working with are great, there's a real mixture. I connect well with some. It's like we're on the same wavelength. With others it's like we're talking past one another . . . like we're talking a foreign language.

This is a book about people. It's a book about relationships. God designed us so that we cannot exist without meaningful interaction with others. In fact, our lives would be sterile without such interaction. But in order to have positive and life-giving relationships, we've got to get along. In some cases, getting along can be quite a challenge.

As we move through the passages of life, we don't experience the same depth of relationship with everyone who crosses our path. For example, we do not have the same kind of relationship with acquaintances at work as with our immediate family. But for some people, their closest relationships *are* at work.

A multitude of factors determine the level of relationship we experience with the people who populate our lives. Sometimes the intensity of a relationship is the result of a planned activity. For instance, you may purposely cultivate a friendship with a new employee or a new person at church in order to make him or her feel included. Sometimes relationships just happen—as in the case of being drawn to someone who enjoys the same hobby you enjoy.

When you spend time in close proximity with others, you will inevitably experience differences of opinion or even outright conflict. Many books have been written on the subject of conflict resolution with the members of our families and with close friends. Do the same principles apply to people at our place of work or with coworkers in volunteer activities, such as church committees and other activities? Absolutely!

OUR SECOND FAMILY

Consider this: Most of us have at least two families. There's a family structure at home, which involves spouse, children and/or parents. But there is also a "family" structure at work, people with whom many of us spend more hours of the day than with our families.

By the way, how many hours a week do you spend at work? Go ahead, write it down. How many hours do you spend commuting? And how many hours do you spend thinking and talking about your work? For some of us, at least half of our waking hours are related to the work environment (and many additional hours are taken up with church activities). Add in time for commuting (sometimes with coworkers who carpool) and work-related tasks while away from work. Don't forget to consider how much time you spend talking about work. Are you surprised at the percentage of time that your life is taken up with work concerns? It's a big chunk, isn't it!

I don't believe it would be an overstatement to say that some of our most important relationships develop through the work environment. You share coffee breaks and lunches with coworkers; you support each other through births, deaths, graduations and marriages; sometimes you even share holidays together. When something bad happens to a coworker, it impacts everyone; and when something good occurs, it's talked about by the others as well. When a worker is upset, it can impact every other person around him. When he or she is absent, it can affect the entire work flow of the office. And when a worker leaves permanently, it leaves a hole in the social structure and can be a major loss for those who were close to the person.

Our lives become a giant series of interactions with the people who share our working hours. That's why we need our work and volunteer work atmosphere to be as conflict-free as possible. We will definitely enjoy our jobs more if we get along with those around us.

Interaction with people is an inescapable fact of life. Yet this inter-action often brings conflict. The logical question then is, How can we minimize the negative aspects of conflict and get along with others on a daily basis? Let's first examine people interaction in light of its capacity to either *deplete* or *replenish* us.

> @
>
> How can we minimize the negative aspects of conflict and get along with others on a daily basis?

KEEPING YOUR BATTERY CHARGED

A depleting relationship causes you to continually draw from your emotional and spiritual reserves in order to cope with its demands. This can happen with parents or a spouse, or with those who join you in volunteer work at church or with those you see every day at your place of employment. Being around a "depleter" is just plain hard work.

Depleters contribute to your problems rather than help you solve them. If you can imagine yourself as a battery, depleters would be the people who drain your battery cells dry. When you're around them for any length of time, it's difficult to have enough juice left to even get started again! I use the term "difficult people" when I talk about depleters. Unfortunately, difficult people are all around us.

Don't get me wrong. There are some wonderful people at your place of work and in your church. You can connect with positive, supportive, caring people in these places and make friendships that last a lifetime. But you will also run into a cast of characters who are a bit different than most. These are the ones who are very difficult to get along with, and most people who encounter them feel the struggle. Difficult people have a way of getting under your skin. They may eventually dominate your thoughts, and you may even dream about them. They can be a huge source of stress in your life.

Difficult people can be psychologically unsound and cause you to feel trapped, abused, demeaned and powerless when you're around them. Their behavior runs the gamut: treating people unfairly, picking on some and treating others with favoritism, stifling some and taking credit for another's accomplishment, demanding that everyone around them become a workaholic as they are, refusing to cooperate and be a member of the team, sabotaging others' efforts—the list goes on. Some difficult people are extremely self-centered, obnoxious and even cruel.

One study indicated that 80 percent of the people surveyed worked with at least one person whose behavior created major stress in their life.[1] That's not a pleasant thought, but it's reality.

Let's face it, when you work with people, there will be problems. There will be conflicts. When a conflict emerges, you have an opportunity to step back and determine the nature of the issue so that you can work to resolve the conflict and minimize the depletion of your emotional and mental reserves. Most conflicts can be divided into five categories.

THE CAUSES OF CONFLICT

Personality

Personality conflicts are at the top of the list. It's possible to resolve a personality conflict by identifying the traits that annoy you or the work patterns with which you clash and then accommodating the other person's trait or style. That is easier to do if you think of the old saying, "Not wrong, just different." Maybe the person's gifts and abilities are mismatched with what is expected of them. Personalities do not change much, so learning to adjust, limiting contact or overlooking some of the issues may lead to resolution.

Goals

There will be conflicts over *goals*. The best solution is to come up with some creative alternatives so that both of you get your needs met. One of the best solutions is for each person to suggest three possible alternatives. When all six are listed, usually it's possible for both to agree upon one. Yes, the solution is different than each intended, but the deadlock is broken and each is satisfied.

Circumstances

Conflicts over *circumstances* are a bit easier to handle. There are all sorts of possibilities for different limits, details or choices. It takes listening and consideration on both sides for resolution to occur. Often negotiation is a big part of the solution. You may not end up with what you originally wanted, but through the process of give-and-take you find a solution.

Facts

Conflict over *facts* can usually be resolved by clarification of the issues, since facts can be verified or refuted. Perhaps there are insufficient details, or the person's style of communication created the conflict in the first place. At any rate, this type of conflict is easy to resolve.

Values

Conflicts over *values* probably will not be resolved. Values reflect who a person is. Values form the basis for how a person looks at other people and how he or she views work, ideas, life, etc. Compromise does not usually work here. Sometimes agreeing to disagree may be the only way to resolve this type of conflict. For a lasting change in values to occur, it takes a life-changing experience with the person of Jesus Christ.

CONFLICTS AT CHURCH

Perhaps in your experience it isn't the people at work who are the most difficult to get along with. Sometimes people in the church aren't who they're supposed to be. The central calling of believers is to love Jesus and others. Love is the message of the Scriptures and it is how we are to live our lives.

> You shall love the LORD your God with all your heart, and with all your soul, and with all your strength, and with all your mind; and your neighbor as yourself (Luke 10:27).

> If I have the gift of prophecy and can fathom all mysteries and all knowledge, and if I have a faith that can move

mountains, but have not love, I am nothing (1 Cor. 13:2, *NIV*).

The one who does not love does not know God, for God is love (1 John 4:8).

Pastor and author John Ortberg, in his outstanding book *Love Beyond Reason: Moving God's Love from Your Head to Your Heart,* talks about people in the church who are sometimes regarded as spiritual giants—even though they damage the Christian image instead of drawing others to Jesus. Have you ever run into people like the ones described below?

He was an angry man—angry toward his children, the people he worked with, the people he had gone to church with his whole life. He got into fights over points of doctrine, over what the sign in front of the church should say, over what the church motto should be.

His main reason to listen to sermons was not to encounter God or be broken by God, but to see where he might be able to point out flaws in them.

People outside the church wouldn't tolerate him because he was obnoxious. Inside the church, though, his obnoxious behavior was regarded as zeal for truth.

She was the most feared person in the church. She was a master at guilt and manipulation. She led a Bible study for women, but it was clear they were welcome only if they'd do what she would say. She was involved in a lot of people's lives but didn't love them. The truth is, she didn't even *like* them.

He is a Christian leader and author who views himself as a defender of the truth. He delights in ripping apart other Christians who disagree with any of his doctrinal positions. He doesn't just oppose their opinions, he caricatures their positions, twists their statements, maligns their motives. He wants to believe bad things about them. He also wants to believe bad things about political figures he disagrees with. He repeats such rumors and spreads them even if he's not sure they're true. He slanders truth in the name of defending truth.

She lived to complain. She complained about her grown children, who did not treat her right, about her neighbors, money, change, and life in general.

When her church went through changes she would oppose them, not so much because she didn't like the change as because changes might mean she was less in control. The changes were opening the church up to unchurchy people she didn't want there, people who didn't look or think or dress or vote like she did.[2]

How do you handle people like these? What's the best way to respond to their behavior? There are times when we need to gently and lovingly confront. But if the people continue on in their ways, it may be best to distance yourself from them. They contaminate the rest of the flock and violate the teachings of Scripture. There may even be times when we need to suggest they leave if they continue to behave in such a way under the guise of being spiritual.

I became acquainted with a young man whose goal in life was to defend the Christian faith and to convince others that it was the only way. Unfortunately, he was one of the most obnoxious individuals I had ever met. I was sorry that he called himself a believer, because it was questionable if his offensive behavior would ever draw a person closer to a relationship with Jesus.

JUST DIFFICULT—OR IMPOSSIBLE?

We've all met impossible people to be around. Some of us even work with them. You know who I'm talking about. Nothing seems to go right with these people. They're "relationship impaired." They just don't respond to interpersonal interactions in the same way others do. They misinterpret, personalize and respond with inappropriate levels of intensity.

What makes people like this such a problem is that they see the way they behave as a strength or a virtue. This is who they want to be! In other words, they are the ones who are normal; you're the one who is difficult. These people are out of step with the rest of the world but they see it in just the opposite way. They're not the ones with the problem. They may actually be proud of the way they are.

We've all met impossible people to be around. Some of us even work with them. They misinterpret, personalize and respond with inappropriate levels of intensity.

Impossible people lack the ability to be emotionally responsive to others. Often these people were raised without an emotional education. They never experienced much empathy themselves, so how could empathy become part of their lives? They are often so caught up in their own world that they really don't give much thought to what others around them are experiencing.

Lack of Boundaries

Boundaries are also foreign to their thinking. They test boundaries constantly by invading or sharing inappropriate information.

If you don't respect boundaries in a working environment, you have a nightmare on your hands.

Did you watch the movie *What About Bob?* If you've seen it, you will know what I'm talking about. This film raises boundary violations to a new level. I didn't like the movie. I was uncomfortable with it because I've seen many people who are like Bob. They often have hidden agendas in the workplace and are inflexible and nonempathetic to the needs of others. Although most of us have learned how to respond to different situations in various ways, this individual responds to life and every nuance of life's experiences in the same way, whether it works or not.[3]

What is the New Testament message about? Part of it is about getting along with others. If you were on a college or professional football team you would have something called the play book. It would be filled with all the various plays you needed and could use to win the game. We do have a play book and it tells us how to win at the game of life. Sure, we wish others would follow these guidelines too. That's a natural wish. But all we have to be concerned with is following the instructions ourselves. Take a look at some of these guidelines and think about how they could be lived out in your life.

Let the peace of Christ rule in your hearts, to which indeed you were called in one body (Col. 3:15).

Be of the same [agreeable] mind one with another; live in peace (2 Cor. 13:11, *AMP*).

So let us then definitely aim for and eagerly pursue what makes for harmony and for mutual upbuilding (edification and development) of one another (Rom. 14:19, *AMP*).

Living as becomes you] with complete lowliness of mind (humility) and meekness (unselfishness, gentleness, mildness), with patience, bearing with one another and making allowances because you love one another (Eph. 4:2, *AMP*).

The Scriptures call us to get along with others. Remember what it says in Romans 12:18, *"If possible*, so far as it depends on you, be at peace with all men." The *New Century* translation says, *"Do your best* to live in peace with everyone" (italics mine). It's interesting to see the qualifiers in this verse—"if possible" and "do your best." Had you ever looked Romans 12:18 in this way?

Sometimes no matter what you do, a person just will not respond in a healthy way. Still, it is vital that you do what you can to maintain peace with him or her.

Keep the guidelines from our Play Book in mind as you journey through the rest of this book. When you follow the principles of Scripture, you grow in your ability to communicate and develop flexibility in your interactions with people. When that happens, you'll be amazed at the relationship changes that can occur.

There is hope that we can all get along much better with others at church and at work. Who wouldn't like that possibility? So where do you begin? With yourself. You'll read about that in the next chapter.

Notes
1. Alan A. Cavaiola, Ph.D. and Neil J. Lavender, Ph.D., *Toxic Coworkers* (Oakland, CA: New Harbinger, 2000), pp. 1-3, adapted.
2. John Ortberg, *Love Beyond Reason* (Grand Rapids, MI: Zondervan Publishers, 1998), pp. 132, 133.
3. Cavaiola and Lavender, *Toxic Coworkers*, pp. 21-28, adapted.

CHAPTER 2

GETTING ALONG WITH OTHERS BEGINS WITH YOU

I'm really involved at my church with groups and a couple of boards. The other day something dawned on me. It's not a whole lot different at church than at work. We've got a mixture of people at both places. I'd like to get along better with a larger group of people. Maybe I could improve the way I communicate with them. Perhaps that's an answer to some of the conflicts.

Improving the way you communicate is a *big* part of the answer to solving relationship conflicts.

How did you learn to get along with others? Did you just come by it naturally? Probably not. Someone taught you or you learned by trial and error. You discovered what works and what doesn't. Most of the responses that didn't work well you left by the wayside. Some you repeated and intensified, refining and perfecting those responses. You began to use them so much that they became part of who you are.

Part of our image is how we react and respond to others. But sometimes our responses are not always the best. I've seen many people who never seem to get the message that the way they try to connect with others just isn't working. Perhaps they sense it to some degree, but instead of making positive changes they intensify their unsuccessful efforts. They seem to lack *flexibility* and *balance* in their lives—two elements that can separate those who get along from those who don't. Flexibility and balance are reflected in the way we communicate.

LIFE IN A SUBMARINE

Have you ever been on the inside of a submarine? I toured a Russian sub built over 40 years ago that was parked next to the Queen Mary in Long Beach, California. What an eye-opener! I'm not claustrophobic, but I wonder how anyone could survive living in those cramped quarters for months at a time and still get along. From what I learned during the tour, there were many who didn't survive emotionally. So the U.S. Navy requested the help of a specialist to determine the most significant qualities to look for in men who could live elbow-to-elbow for long periods of time in the hot, smelly, cramped quarters of a submarine.

Many qualities were discovered, but three qualities were given more significance than others. As we discuss these qualities, imagine your work or church environment in terms of a small cramped tube called a submarine. Perhaps the significance of these qualities will take on new meaning for you.

Inclusion
One factor necessary to survive life in close proximity with others is *inclusion*. What comes to mind when you think of this word?

Inclusion is the level at which we like to include people in our lives. It's also the level at which we like to be included in the lives of others.

What is your preference at work? Do you prefer to be close to a few people or to many, and do you become close to a few or to many at *their* invitation? Inclusion simply measures the breadth and depth of friends you choose and accept.

Some people prefer to invite others into their lives but don't respond to invitations. Some prefer to respond to the overtures of others but don't initiate invitations. What about you? What people have you invited into your life and who are the people you have responded to? If you're only an includer and not a responder, especially at work, what effect do you think this would have on relationships over time? If you're just the opposite, what effect might this have over time?

Whether you include and respond to a multitude of people or to a select few (the reason for many or few could be your personality type), a balance between the two qualities is most desirable for healthy relationships.

Control

A second factor important to surviving life up close and personal is *control*. Some individuals exercise quite a bit of influence, or leadership, whereas others are content to follow and are willing to be influenced by others. People will feel comfortable with you if they know where you stand on this issue—if they know whether you are either an influencer or a follower.

I've seen a number of people at work and at church who shift back and forth between leading and following, depending on the setting and the amount of investment or interest they have in the situation. If there is no discernible reason for the shift, then problems arise. Predictability provides security for many.

Effect

The third characteristic is *effect*. This is the level at which we get close to people and the level at which we allow them to get close to us. Being close to another person requires openness, vulnerability and transparency. In other words, you cannot wear a mask.

Some people are selective, choosing to be close to a few people and allowing only a few to get close to them. Others let many people get close to them. When you are open, your motivations can be understood to a greater degree.

As in the case with inclusion, problems arise when either openness or closeness is the only way you connect with people. Again, a healthy balance between the two is best.

Inclusion is not the same as effect. You may be connected to many people, but if the effect is low, there is little closeness.

Whom have you chosen to get close to and allowed to get close to you? Are there as many people as you would like? Who else at work or church would you like to be closer to? If you can think of no one, why is that? Is there a balance in this area of your life?

The combination of these three areas—inclusion, control and effect—are what we call *interpersonal style*. It is not really a personality trait. We will examine personality traits in greater depth later in the book.[1] If you haven't been successful in your relationships, your interpersonal style can be altered by learning new patterns of relating to others.

EMOTIONAL BANK ACCOUNT

If you've done much reading in the area of marriage relationships, I'm sure you've come across the concept of the *emotional bank account*. Several writers have emphasized its importance in building a quality marriage. If the principle can be effective in a marriage, why not in our other relationships?

We all know what a financial bank account is. In my bank account I make periodic deposits and build up a reserve. Then I make a withdrawal when I need to. Now transfer that concept to an emotional bank account—a simple metaphor that describes the amount of trust we build up in our relationships with people.

When you make deposits into someone's emotional bank account through courtesy, kindness, honesty, sensitivity, attention and keeping your commitments, you build up a reserve with them. The other person's trust toward you grows and you can call upon that trust many times when needed. When you make mistakes or are not consistent with your positive input, the emotional reserve will compensate for it. This is such an important principle for the communication process. When the trust account is high, communication is more effective. Even when you're not clear in your communication or when you're not that communicative on an off day, the other person responds with "Oh yeah, I know what he really means." When you've built a good track record with someone, there's a greater understanding and acceptance of you.

What happens if you're not consistent with your positive responses or if your pattern of behavior tends to be just the opposite—manifesting discourtesy, criticism, threats, silence, neglect or control? In time (and not too long a time) the emotional bank accounts of those around you will be overdrawn. Trust diminishes. Others are less inclined to listen to you, to comply, to follow or to cooperate. Toleration may be their main response, and tension may cloud the atmosphere. Trust diminishes in any relationship if a person does not continue to make regular deposits.

Assume for a minute that you own the Bank of Trust. And assume that those with whom you are closest at work and at church (the ones you need to interact with on a regular basis) are your depositors. Who makes the largest deposit to your bank? What do they deposit? How do you respond to your biggest depositors compared to those who just barely keep the balance from being overdrawn? Aren't you more open, accepting, understanding and trusting toward the big depositors? And aren't you a bit wary and cautious toward those who tend to overdraw? It's the same way in our relationships.

What kind of depositor are you? What balance would your bank account with others show? *The more difficult the communication issues, the more of a positive balance we need in the bank of trust.* And the deposits need to be made on a regular basis. This is not a money market account that you can dump a lot into once a year and then draw on all year. It must be consistently fed.[2]

The Currency of Understanding

What are some deposits you could make in your relationships with those at work, at church or even in the neighborhood? One of the most important deposits is making the decision to take the time to understand those around you.

A foundational biblical verse of Scripture for family relationships is Ephesians 4:2, *AMP*: "Living as becomes you with complete lowliness of mind (humility) and meekness (unselfishness, gentleness, mildness), with patience, bearing with one another *and* making allowances because you love one another."

To me "bearing with and making allowances" can mean understanding, accepting, adapting and being flexible. In other words, our calling is to understand other people, accept who they are and learn to be flexible and adapt to their uniqueness. In terms of the theme of this book, it means learning to communicate in such a way that you are able to connect with people by learning to speak their language.

Understanding a person has to occur before you can build a relationship. You don't know what makes up a deposit for another person until you understand them. Therefore, the definition of a deposit for one person may not be a deposit for another.

In order to make a deposit to someone's emotional account, you need to discover what is important to that person; and it

In order to make a deposit to someone's emotional account, you need to discover what is important to that person and it needs to become as important to you.

needs to become as important to *you*. For instance, if a co-worker says, "I really need you to listen to this alternative suggestion I've been thinking about," your deposit comes by stopping what you're doing and really listening, without interrupting. When you do that, you have accepted and validated what is important to your coworker.

We cannot determine what is important to another person. If we do that, we will base our conclusions on our own needs and desires. I've seen in-dividuals in families, work and church situations try time and again to make deposits, but the deposits never get posted. These people failed to understand the other person's need.

The Currency of Dependability

Another major deposit in the trust bank account is dependabili-ty. Keeping your commitments is an expression of dependability. Today's promises seem to be made and broken with great ease.

The word "commit" is a verb that means "to do or perform." A commitment is a binding pledge or promise that is not based on feelings. In marriage, commitment is likened to bungee jumping. If you've ever taken the plunge, you know that when you take that step off the platform, you are committed to follow through. There's no more time to think it over or change your mind. There's no turning back.

It may be wise to always take time for some thoughtful consideration before making a commitment. When you are a person of your word, others confide in you, seek your opinion and are drawn to you. Your dependability may be the open door for you to talk about your faith with someone who doesn't as yet have a faith relationship with Jesus Christ.

The Currency of Integrity

Another big deposit is integrity. If this is lacking, it can undermine any other effort to build trust. Lack of integrity can actually negate the effect of other deposits.

How would you define the word "integrity"? Some say, "Well, if you have integrity, you're an honest person." Some equate this quality with honesty, but it goes beyond that. Author Steven Covey describes honesty as "telling the truth that is conforming our words to reality."[3] Integrity is conforming reality to our words. You keep promises and fulfill expectations. You work at matching your words, feelings, thoughts and actions. You're the real thing—you're authentic. You don't have any desire to deceive.

We are quite sensitive about this issue of integrity, especially with what we've seen in political leaders and, unfortunately, even with some leaders in ministry.

If you are a person of integrity, you treat every person in a consistent manner by the same set of principles, whether or not they are in your presence. Integrity means you do not belittle, criticize, gossip or betray confidences. There is no subtle or overt deception involved in what you do or say.[4]

Psalm 15 describes how to live a life of integrity:

LORD, who may go and find refuge and shelter in your tabernacle up on your holy hill? Anyone who leads a blameless life and is truly sincere. Anyone who refuses to slander others, does not listen to gossip, never harms his neighbor, speaks out against sin, criticizes those committing it, commends the faithful followers of the Lord, keeps a promise even if it ruins him, does not crush his debtors with high interest rates, and refuses to testify against the innocent despite the bribes offered him— such a man shall stand firm forever (Psalm 15, *TLB*).

Consider what Sam Storms said about integrity:

1. A person of integrity fulfills his or her promises. Being true to one's word, especially when doing so is costly (in terms of money, convenience, physical welfare, and so on), is a core characteristic of integrity.
2. A person of integrity speaks the truth, is honest, and does not lie.
3. A person of integrity is a person of sincerity. This is to say, a person of integrity hates hypocrisy.
4. A person of integrity manifests a wholeness of character, including kindness, compassion, mercy, and gentleness.
5. A person of integrity is committed to the pursuit and maintenance of justice and fairness.
6. A person of integrity loves as, when, and what God loves.
7. A person of integrity is humble. He or she shuns pride and haughtiness.
8. A person of integrity is law-abiding. He or she plays by the rules, both in the Bible and the law of the land.
9. A person of integrity is fundamentally altruistic. That is to say, he is committed not simply to laws and rules but to people. Could a selfish person have much integrity? What about someone who is honest, law-abiding, and fulfills his or her promises but is self-absorbed and egocentric? Does the latter eliminate the possibility of integrity?
10. A person of integrity manifests a high degree of consistency. That is to say, he or she is not always changing

the principles on the basis of which they live, unless compelled to do so by the Bible or rational persuasion.[5]

The Currency of Honor

A deposit that is frequently overlooked as well as deficient in many relationships is honor. This sounds different, doesn't it? Honor? Why honor? First Peter 2:17 tells us to "Honor all." What does this mean?

The word "honor" in Greek means "to highly value, to prize, to not take lightly, to esteem, to give weight to, to ascribe worth." It is significant that the word "glory" in the Old and New Testaments often shares the same definition as the word "honor."

The Bible gives us three levels of honor that are applied to man. The first level is intrinsic honor. It is honor possessed by God and given to every human being. This honor is an attribute of God and He freely bestows it on us simply by creating us in His image. The second level is honor based on character. The third level of honor is based on performance.

One author wrote:

To honor is to have great respect. When we honor others, we respect them, we trust them, we believe in them. We tend to hold those who are honest and manifest integrity in their beliefs and actions in high esteem. A man or woman of honor has unquestionable integrity and dependability.

According to the dictionary, honor is uprightness; living with the highest moral principles; having an absence of deceit or fraud; adhering to the truth. Honor connotes a fine sense of, and strict conformity to, what is considered right, especially in business dealings. Honor is uncompromising honesty and trustworthiness, a sound or moral principle which no power or influence can impair. Honor suggests a combination of liking and respect, deference, homage, reverence, and veneration.[6]

Honoring another person can help to change his life, whether he wants to change or not. It's easy to honor an honorable person, but honoring the pain in the neck is another thing. When you do honor him, look at what can happen. Author Fawn Parish tells of her experience in this regard:

> Quite a few years ago I worked for a man who was so difficult he was borderline impossible. No one in the entire company could please him. He was an angry, bitter man who spat out disdain like some men spit tobacco. All the employees in the company sought to avoid him, but because he owned the company, there was really no place to hide. Christians were repugnant to him. Knowing that I was a Christian, he intentionally hired me for a sparring partner.
>
> One day I found myself facing him and doing a curious thing. I honored him. I honored him by telling him some things I'd observed about him. I said, 'You know, I've figured out three things about you. You're a teacher, you love knowledge and you have little patience for those who don't.' He gave me a startled look. No one had ever noticed that about him before. But I didn't make it up. All of it happened to be true, and he knew it.
>
> God opened a small door to my boss's heart through that simple conversation.[7]

The Currency of Attitude

Everyone has an attitude. You know what that is, don't you? It's your way of thinking, feeling or perceiving something.

We've been talking about the emotional bank account and making deposits into others' accounts. But have you ever considered making a deposit into your own account? We do it all the time, but most deposits are automatic, such as when we talk to ourselves. Yes, you talk to yourself! And so do I.

Have you ever caught yourself making an internal statement and then wondering where *that* came from? Some of what you say to yourself reflects your belief and attitude about yourself. But not only that, it also *creates* your attitude toward yourself. If what you say is negative, limiting or self-depreciating, it affects how you respond to others and makes you less likely to communicate at your best or to present yourself in the best way possible. You also do not have as much energy as you need to respond in a healthy manner to others. Your energy has been used to deal with how you feel about yourself because of your internal messages.

You cannot control what another person thinks, says or does; but you can control two things: what you say to yourself about yourself and how you respond to what others say about you and do to you. Think about these questions for a minute:

When you think about yourself, are you hard on yourself or do you think about yourself in a fair manner?

How does your attitude about yourself affect how you get along with others at work or at church?

Who is in charge of your attitude?

There are five messages in what you say: What you mean to say, what you actually said, what the other person hears, what the other person thinks he heard, what the other person says about what you said.

The Currency of Listening

Another deposit (which will be amplified in another chapter) is to listen to others. One of the main reasons a person is drawn to someone is because he is being listened to.

Time is another basic deposit behind the gift of listening. You cannot listen—you will not listen—unless you take the time. When you respond to someone because he or she is listening to you, remember that what is being given to you is more than just hearing what you have to say—that other person is putting on hold whatever else is occurring in his or her life and is saying, "Right now, whatever is happening in the universe is secondary to you. What you have to say takes precedence over everything else. This time is yours."

Have you ever looked at listening in this way? Try to see your act of listening as a gift of time and a major deposit to another person's emotional bank account.

Another way of helping to assure that you're making a deposit is to become an auditor. Perhaps you've been in a company when an audit has occurred. Those who are involved in examining and verifying accounts are very meticulous and thorough in what they do. We need to become auditors in the selection of the words we use in our interactions with others. So often what we mean to say is not what comes out, or we need to correct what we intended to say since it could hurt a person rather than end up as a positive deposit. Communication is not just opening your mouth and letting words flow out. It's more complex than that.

There are five messages in what you say:

what you mean to say
what you actually said
what the other person hears
what the other person thinks he heard
what the other person says about what you said

Perhaps a couple of verses in Proverbs should be the guide for our lives in this manner of auditing our words:

Those who are careful about what they say keep themselves out of trouble (Prov. 21:23, *NCV*).

Do you see people who speak too quickly? There is more hope for a foolish person than for them (Prov. 29:20, *NCV*).

We all want what we say to be an asset and not a liability. But it takes time and effort to overcome the improper presentation of our words.

The Currency of Encouragement

One major deposit that is too often lacking is encouragement.

To be an encourager you need to have an attitude of optimism. The *American Heritage Dictionary* gives one of the better definitions of the word: "a tendency or disposition to expect the best possible outcome, or to dwell on the most hopeful aspect of a situation." When this is your attitude or perspective, you will be able to encourage others. Encouragement is "to inspire; to continue on a chosen course; to impart courage or confidence."

Encouragement is sometimes thought of as praise and reinforcement, but it is also much more that that. Praise is limited; it is a verbal reward. It emphasizes competition, has to be earned and is often given for being the best. On the other hand, encouragement is not a response to performance; it is freely given. It can involve noticing what others take for granted and affirming something that others notice but may never think of mentioning.

Encouragement is recognizing the other person as having worth and dignity. It means paying attention to them when they are sharing with you. It means listening in a way that lets them know they are being listened to.

Encouragement validates what a person does or says. It lets people know they matter to you. When you encourage, you respect a person. You rephrase negatives into positives by discovering the constructive elements in situations, such as identifying strengths and focusing on a person's efforts and contributions.[8] This means you find something of value to recognize when everybody else has despaired. Encouragement builds up!

When you encourage someone, you are also saying that you expect the best of him or her. Consider what happened to this young man because his high school principal expected something more from him:

I remember vividly the day we had a school assembly. Three buddies and I went out behind the school auditorium. We all lit up. We knew we were safe; everyone else was in the assembly. And then, who should come around the corner but the principal. We were caught red-handed. My friends took off in three directions and left me just standing there. The principal collared me and dragged me down the hall in front of the auditorium just as the assembly was letting out. I thought I was going to die. Hundreds of kids saw me in this humiliating situation.

He took me into his office and chewed me out royally. It felt as if it lasted forever. Maybe it was only ten or fifteen minutes. I couldn't wait to get out of there. From that time on, I hated this guy. I waited for him to nail my buddies, but he never did. He knew who they were, but he did nothing. One day I saw him in the hall, and I asked why he hadn't gone after them. It wasn't fair that I was singled out.

Instead of giving me an answer there, he grabbed me by the collar and dragged me back into his office. He sat me down, but the chewing out didn't even last a minute this time. I'll never forget what he said, "I wish your friends the best. I don't know what's going to happen to them, but you could be somebody. I expect more of you than this. You're coasting through life. When are you going to do something with what you've got?" He turned around and walked out. I felt like I had been slapped across the face. He was right; I was coasting. And there is only one direction you can coast—down.

I was a junior at the time. I started working a little bit in my classes and made a new group of friends. My senior year I had an A average. I had been getting C's and D's before. I decided I wanted to go on to college, but when I applied, I couldn't get in. My grades were too bad in a previous term. My principal wrote a letter of recommendation on my behalf, and in response the university agreed to admit me on a probationary status. I chose the field I did because of this man. He became like a mentor, like a second father to me.

Two years ago I gave the eulogy at his funeral. I'll never forget him. I will always be different because of him. He gave me something to live up to.[9]

John Maxwell, in his book *Be a People Person*, says we need to anticipate that others will do their best: "When working with people I always try to look at them not as they are but as what they can be. By anticipating that the vision will become real, it's easy for me to encourage them as they stretch. Raise your anticipation level and you raise their achievement level."[10]

Perhaps one of the best ways to describe encouragement is through the example of gardening. I've raised flowers and vegetables for years. Some years were good; others I'd rather forget! At times I've raised tomatoes. Now there's a right way to raise tomatoes and a wrong way. The right way is to make sure you have good soil with plenty of nutrients. You need water, cultivation and fertilizers in the right amounts. You also need to stake the plant or use round wire cages for them to grow on. They need this support or their branches break. Sometimes you need to put up a protective cover and, above all, watch out for insects, especially tomato worms.

After you've done all this, you can take several weeks off to do nothing, right? No, you have to care for tomato plants consistently rather than sporadically, or you won't produce a crop. Encouragement is like this. It takes work—constant, consistent work—to be effective.[11]

When you are an encourager, you're like a prospector or a deep-sea diver looking for hidden treasure. Every person has pockets of underdeveloped resources within them. Your task is to search for these pockets, discover them and expand them. As you discover the strengths, you will begin to focus on them. You will look at the person and care about what you discover. At first your discovery may be rough and imperfect. Talent scouts and scouts for professional sports teams do this all the time. They see undeveloped raw talent, but they also see potential.

Look at what God's Word tells us to do in the matter of encouragement. In Acts 18:27, the word "encourage" means to urge forward or persuade. In 1 Thessalonians 5:11 it means to stimulate another person to the ordinary duties of life.

Consider the words found in 1 Thessalonians 5:14 (*AMP*):

> Every person has pockets of underdeveloped resources within them. When you are an encourager, you're like a prospector or a deep-sea diver looking for hidden treasure.

And we earnestly beseech you, brethren, admonish (warn and seriously advise) those who are out of line [the loafers, the disorderly and the unruly]; encourage the timid and fainthearted, help and give your support to the weak souls [and] be very patient with everybody [always keeping your temper].

Scripture uses a variety of words to describe both our involvement with others as well as the actual relationship. The word "urge" (*parakaleo)* means to beseech or exhort. It is intended to create an environment of urgency to listen and respond to a directive. Paul used it in Romans 12:1 and in 1 Corinthians 1:10.

The words translated "encourage" (*paramutheomai)* mean to console, comfort, and cheer up. This process includes elements of understanding, redirecting of thoughts and a general shifting of focus from the negative to the positive. In the context of the verse, encourage refers to the timid ("fainthearted," *AMP*) individual who is discouraged and ready to give up. It's a matter of loaning your faith and hope to the person until his own develops.

The word "help" *(anechomai)* primarily contains the idea of taking interest in, being devoted to, rendering assistance or holding up spiritually and emotionally. It is not so much an active involvement as a passive approach. It suggests the idea of coming alongside a person and supporting him. In the context of 1 Thessalonians 5:14, it seems to refer to those who are incapable of helping themselves.

First Thessalonians 5:11 (*NIV*) states, "Therefore encourage one another and build each other up, just as in fact you are doing."

Hebrews 3:13 says we are to encourage one another every day. In the setting of this verse, encouragement is associated with protecting the believer from callousness.

Hebrews 10:25 (*NIV*) says, "Let us encourage one another." This time the word means to keep someone on their feet who, if left to himself, would collapse. Your encouragement serves like the concrete pilings of a structural support.

True Encouragement
Consider this parable from Scripture put into a modern context. Perhaps you've met each of the four characters. Which of the four would best describe *your* response to people in need?

A young man ran out of gas one hot afternoon in the middle of a desert in Arizona. He was too far from civilization to walk for help, so his only hope was that a passing motorist would stop and lend him aid. Unfortunately, passing motorists were few and far between on this isolated stretch of desert highway. The young man sat dejectedly in his car and prayed that some caring soul would pass his way.

Eventually, a car did appear down that lonely ribbon of road. To the young man's great joy, the driver saw his plight and pulled up beside him. He inquired as to the young man's problem, and when he heard it was lack of gasoline he launched into a scholarly discussion of the various kinds of gasoline available. It was obvious that this driver was schooled in the chemical properties of gasoline and spoke authoritatively of octane levels and the difference between leaded and unleaded fuel. After delivering his impressive discourse and prescribing the ideal fuel for the young man's car, he went merrily on his way. As he pulled away, the young man noticed the personalized plates on his car: T-H-I-N-K-E-R.

An hour or so passed and a second car pulled over. The driver was meek and kind and, upon hearing the problem, offered assuring words of comfort. He expressed genuine concern for the young man's dilemma and then intoned a lengthy prayer on his behalf. He asked

God to smile upon this difficult situation and to fill the empty gas tank with fuel from heaven. Then he got back in his car and sped down the highway. As the young man watched the car pull away, he saw printed on the license plate this word: P-R-A-Y-E-R. The young man slumped despondently in his car.

To his surprise and delight, however, a third car pulled alongside him in just a matter of minutes. The driver jumped out, quickly ascertained the young man's plight and launched into an animated exhortation. First he chided him for his carelessness, then outlined a four-point program for driving a car successfully. When he finished, he too took off down the road. The bewildered young man saw that his license plate read: P-E-R-S-U-A-D-E-R.

In despair the young man looked up and down the desert highway. An hour passed. No cars came into view. All the young man could do was wait—and hope against hope that help would come.

Finally, a fourth car approached. The young man's heart did flip-flops as the car pulled up next to his. The driver inquired as to the problem and then pulled a five-gallon gas can from his trunk. He emptied the contents of the can into the young man's tank and waited until he was sure the car would start. Then, smiling, he went on his way. The young man hardly had time to shout a thank-you. He did glimpse the car's license plates, but they were not personalized and he couldn't quite make out the letters. With great gratitude and relief, the young man shifted his car into gear and rumbled down the highway.[12]

The marines advertise that they are looking for a few good men. Jesus is looking for more than a few. He wants all of us to live in such a way that we bring out the best in others and draw them to Him. Being different by manifesting understanding, dependability, integrity, honor toward others, a positive attitude, a listening ear and, finally, being known as an encourager will allow you to get along well with others. And even more importantly, you may influence them to consider Jesus as their Lord and Savior. What could be any better than that?

Notes

1. Charles J. Keating, *Dealing with Difficult People* (New York: Paulist Press, 1984), pp. 22-29, adapted.
2. Stephen R. Covey, *The Seven Habits of Highly Effective People* (New York: Simon and Schuster, 1989), pp. 188, 189, adapted.
3. Ibid., p. 195.
4. Ibid., p. 196, adapted.
5. Sam Storms, *Pleasures Evermore* (Colorado Springs, CO: NavPress, 2000), pp. 245, 246.
6. Blaine Lee, *The Power Principle* (New York: Simon and Schuster, 1997), p. 109.
7. Fawn Parish, *Honor: What Love Looks Like* (Ventura, CA.: Renew Books, 1999), p. 137.
8. Robert Sherman, Paul Oresky, and Yvonne Roundtree, *Solving Problems in Couples and Family Therapy* (New York: Bruner Mazel, 1991), pp. 27, 28, adapted.
9. Blaine Lee, *The Power Principle*, pp. 161, 162.
10. John C. Maxwell, *Be a People Person* (Wheaton, IL: Victor Books, 1994), p. 137.
11. Blaine Lee, *The Power Principle*, pp. 125, 126.
12. Judson Edwards, *Regaining Control of Your Life* (Minneapolis, MN: Bethany House Publishers, 1989), pp. 90, 91.

CHAPTER 3

ARE THEY DIFFICULT OR IMPOSSIBLE?

The other day I was walking to the staff room for a break. As I got closer I could
hear Jim's voice lashing out at someone. I tell you, my stomach turned sour!
I could have gone all day (or all month) without running into Attila the Hun.
I decided my waistline didn't need the donut and I'd had too much coffee
already, so I did an about-face and went back to my office. I alerted two others
who were on their way into the staff room and they changed their minds as
well. I don't care who you are, this guy is impossible to get along with.

There are scary people out there. I call these Level II people. Level
I are the everyday, somewhat normal, folks like us!

DIFFICULT PEOPLE

Many of these Level II people are what Les Parrott terms *high
maintenance* people. You'll find them everywhere. What's their

problem? Maybe they think they know it all or maybe they won't cooperate or ever admit they've made a mistake. Or maybe they aren't team players.

As you read this chapter, keep in mind two questions: Do I know someone who fits this description? (And are you praying for this person?) Do I fit any of these descriptions? (If so, it would be beneficial to read Les Parrott's book *High Maintenance Relationships*). He has identified several types of high-maintenance people:

The *critic*—self-appointed complainer who is constantly chipping away at others.

The *martyr*—always the victim and full of self-pity.

The *pessimist*—the one who sees the glass half-empty: "It will never work."

The *steam roller*—the one who doesn't know the meaning of the word tact. Their comments hurt but they don't care.

The *gossiper*—who is filled with envy.

The *taker*, the *workaholic* and the *controller*.[1]

None of these types is a biblical pattern for how to live. But you've probably got some of them in your life whether you want them there or not. You may be interacting with them in your neighborhood, your place of work or at church. Whenever you have identified people as difficult, ask yourself these questions:

• To what degree *must* I be involved with this person?
• To what degree do I *need* to be involved with this person?
• To what degree do I *want* to be involved with this person?

Your responses to the first two questions will reveal that you may need to make adjustments in order to get along. Remember that getting along may not mean a deep level of involvement but rather a more accepting, understanding and pleasant interaction. By the way, difficult people can change. You'll read about that later.

If you discover that you don't have to be, need to be or want to be involved with that difficult person, the solution is fairly obvious. It's all right *not* to want to be involved with some people. We can't and won't connect with everyone.

On the other hand, some people are more than difficult to get along with. These are the Level II people. *Warning:* This next group is dangerous to your emotional health.

"Emotional vampires" might look better than most people. You end up liking them, trusting them and expecting more from them than from others. But eventually you end up being drained dry.

IMPOSSIBLE PEOPLE

Two books released in 2000 were *Toxic Coworkers* and *Emotional Vampires—Dealing with People Who Drain You Dry.* The books describe people who masquerade as regular people but turn into predators and tap your emotional energy. At first they might look better than most people. You end up liking them, trusting them, and expecting more from them than from others. But eventually you end up being drained dry.

The term *emotional vampire* is used for those who have characteristics of what is usually called *personality disorder*. They are not folks who drive themselves crazy; they drive others crazy! Oh, they do have characteristics that others find attractive, but they also cause the greatest amount of difficulty for most of us at work, church, the neighborhood or even in the family. I've seen them operate in every one of these arenas. Some emotional vampires have a lesser degree of intensity of a particular characteristic, while others are walking textbooks of the disorder.

The level of immaturity on their part relates to the degree in which they function without consideration of how their behavior affects others. You are simply there to be used for what they need at the moment. It's important that you learn to recognize impossible people. Some people are just difficult and annoying. Not so with emotional vampires. They're dangerous, even though at times they seem normal. Do you think this description is too strong? Listen to what the authors of *Toxic Coworkers* have to say:

> Like a hidden cancer, personality disorders gradually infect the entire body of the organization, undetected and proliferating. We believe that at the root of the stickiest personnel problems there lies an undetected, insidious personality disorder. We realize that this is a strong statement to make. But we believe it is all too true. The financial costs of this problem are enormous but the personal damage to those employees who must interact with a personality-disorder coworker are incalculable.[2]

What are emotional vampires like? They believe their needs are more important than yours, no matter what. Rules apply to others, not to them. It's never their fault; their motives are pure. They don't wait, since they have no impulse control. And if they don't get their way, watch out, since you've never seen a tantrum like they can throw. They are confused about their own identities. Integrity is a foreign concept to them.

"Clever" is a key word to remember, since most impossible people have the ability to turn themselves into what you want to see in order to get what they want. If an emotional vampire offers to help you or give you something, watch out. You're being set up. They know how to control you.

Can they be classified or given descriptive terms? Yes, but the few disorders mentioned here are the ones you are likely to have little effect upon. However, you can learn how to survive interaction with them.

Narcissism

Have you heard the term "narcissist"? *Narcissists* believe that life revolves around them. Many of them are quite talented, but they are never as great as they believe they are. What they do best is focus upon themselves; what they don't do is have any concern for the needs, thoughts and feelings of others. They are absorbed with themselves. Even when they become Christians, many narcissists distort their faith to fit what they want.

They constantly call attention to themselves in one way or another. They are experts at making the right impression. They want your attention, adulation and worship. They will recount achievements and experiences you never asked them about. You probably see them as conceited. If you work with a narcissist at your place of employment or at church, you may feel ambivalent about them if they're really good at what they do.

Narcissists have fantasies about how great they are and feel they are special; therefore, rules do not apply to them. They compete only when they can win; they can't accept criticism; and they have no concern for you. As a friend of mine said, "They're legends in their own minds."

Do you know anyone like this? If so, what has been your experience with him or her? How do you get along? How has this person impacted your church, work or organization? Have you ever held some of their beliefs at one time, even to a small degree? Have you ever wanted to promote or actually promoted yourself as an expert? Probably. It could be that we have all done this to a degree. But can you imagine someone who is consumed by this belief and behavior system? And can you imagine the disruption this person can bring into the lives of others?[3]

Antisocial Behavior

Another clever type of person is the *antisocial* type. Persons of this type are the most dangerous. They crave excitement, a good time and immediate gratification of their needs. They have little conscience development. The old term we used for the antisocial was "sociopath."

Antisocial people are involved with others but they don't connect with them. They don't know how to connect. They are loners as well as predators. Unfortunately, they can package this aberrant behavior so well that you are fooled. They can be real charmers. You end up being convinced they have what you want.

Day-to-day rules do not apply to them. They are risk-takers, often at your expense. Many people have been conned by this type since they can be so convincing.[4]

Why talk about the antisocial personality disorder in a Christian book? Aren't most of these individuals nonbelievers and out there in the world? No, they are everywhere. I've seen them in "Christian" businesses, on church committees and even in the role of pastor. They know how to speak the language. If you're around one of them for long enough you begin to pick up inconsistencies between what they do and what they say.

A number of years ago I made an interesting discovery while teaching a graduate course in biblical integration. We were doing an exhaustive study on the book of Proverbs and had focused on every passage that described the fool and the scoffer. As we listed these descriptions on a chart, several of us began to sense that we had seen this listing before. We went back to an Abnormal Psychology text and read the description of the anti-social personality. The similarities were amazing. In the commentary on Proverbs by Derek Kidner we read:

> He likes his folly, going back to it "like a dog that returns to his vomit" (26:11); he has no reverence for truth, preferring comfortable illusions (see 14:8).
>
> In society the fool is, in a word, a menace. At best, he wastes your time: "you will not find a word of sense in him" (14:7); and he may be a more serious nuisance. If he has an idea in his head, nothing will stop him: "let a bear robbed of her whelps meet a man, rather than a fool in his folly" (17:12)—whether that folly is some prank that is beyond a joke (10:23), or some quarrel he must pick (18:6) and run to death (29:11). Give him a wide berth, for "the companion of fools shall smart for it" (13:20).
>
> The fool gives himself away as soon as he opens his mouth (see 17:28; 24:7; cf. 10:14), and he is as quarrelsome as his other self—for he knows no restraint (see 20:3; 12:16) and has no sense of proportion (see 27:3; 29:9). The feature that seems specially prominent is his moral insolence: from his first appearance onwards he is impatient of all advice (see 1:7; 10:8; 12:15; 15:5), and his flippant outlook is crystallized in the famous phrase, "fools make a mock at sin" (14:9).
>
> The scoffer or scorner makes about seventeen appearances in the book, and is contrasted with the wise. He shares with his fellows their strong dislike of correction (see 9:7,8; 13:1; 15:12), and it is this, not any lack of intelligence, that blocks any move he makes towards wisdom (see 14:6). The mischief he does is not the random mischief of the ordinary fool, but the deeper damage of the "debunker" and the deliberate trouble-maker (see 21:24;

22:10; 29:8). He impresses the impressionable, as long as he is allowed his way (see 19:25; 21:11).[5]

Do you know anyone like this? If so, what has been your experience with this person? How has this person impacted your church, work or organization?

High Drama

Have you ever been around the person who just has to have approval and attention? Many of these people seem to have what it takes to get it—wit, enthusiasm, conversational skills—it's all there along with the dramatic. Unfortunately the dramatic is all you get—it's a show with little depth. We call these individuals *histrionic* (which is a more accurate name than the old term "hysterical"). They can be men or women, but are usually the latter. A histrionic's world is in a state of upheaval. Histrionics can be alert and happy one moment and down in the dumps the next if they don't perceive themselves as perfect. Oh, they put on a good show, but what you see is not what you get.

Socially speaking, this person can connect. Histrionics love other people, and most of the time you'll enjoy their company. If you interact at church or at work with a histrionic and you don't give them enough attention (their need is insatiable!), they will trot down the hall to find anyone who will put the spotlight on them. Boundaries do not seem to exist when they need attention. They will do whatever it takes to get it, and they need the attention to be positive. As one histrionic shared with me, "I just want everyone to think I'm wonderful!" You can see how this drive can interfere with issues at work or at church. Have you ever left a flower out of water? It shrivels up and dies, doesn't it? This is the histrionic without positive attention.

What world do these people live in? The world of emotions. They define reality by what they feel. What they think or know doesn't count. Internally they experience little feeling of competency. They are quite dependent and their show is to get someone to take care of them and rescue them. Do looks matter? You bet they do, and histrionics spare no time or cost to achieve a good appearance. Backbone? Not really. They have the ability to flex and mold themselves into whatever you want if it brings them attention.

Unfortunately, because they seem to have selective memories, remembering only what will aid them, they have little insight into what they are doing.[6]

Other Personality Disorders

These three descriptions of personality disorders are just the tip of the iceberg in terms of the complete description of the emotional vampire and are representative of numerous other types you will encounter. You need to be aware of these people. Most likely you will work with them, serve with them on committees or fellowship with them at church.

For instance, there are people who do not care for any closeness with others. For them, friendship does not exist. They have no understanding of people or their needs. We call them *schizoid*.

The *paranoid* person is irrationally fearful and suspicious of others—likely to see a conspiracy behind every bush. And this personality disorder comes in varying degrees of paranoia.

If you find someone who is unable to have stable and sane relationships with others and has a magical way of disrupting your life, this may be a *borderline* personality. You'll see this one in the movie *Fatal Attraction*. Borderline personalities have been described as *a storm in every port*. If a borderline is your boss, coworker or employee, hang on tight to the safety bar of your roller coaster car.

There are other personality disorders that are not as volatile, such as the *obsessive compulsive*. This person must always be right and must do everything perfectly but cares little for emotional propriety. There is also the *avoidant*, who is afraid of taking any risk for a relationship; the *dependent*, who can't make personal decisions; and the *passive aggressive*, who will get you, but not in an obvious way.[7]

INTERACTING WITH IMPOSSIBLE PEOPLE

What can you do when rubbing elbows with a person who is narcissistic, antisocial or histrionic—or with any of the other personality disorders described?

For a number of years the action-packed police television show *Hill Street Blues* captivated viewers. This precinct was occupied by a motley group of characters. In fact, you weren't sure as a viewer if you'd even want their help!

Every day a briefing took place. The atmosphere was often chaotic and disruptive. But just before dismissing the rowdy officers, the sergeant would pause and say, "Let's be careful out there!" He was warning them to be alert, to keep their guard up and to never slack off, because the unpredictable could and would happen.

To be careful means to be wary, to keep your eyes open, to be alert. Let your guard down just once and you may do something that will cause great harm. That is why the same caution is repeated throughout the Scriptures. Listen to these warnings:

Be careful that you don't fall (1 Cor. 10:12, *NIV*).

Be very careful, then, how you live (Eph. 5:15, *NIV*).

Be careful that none of you be found to have fallen short (Heb. 4:1, *NIV*).

Remember, there's a reason for all the warnings. Who are the people you need to be most careful around?

Think back over the brief descriptions of the avoidant, the dependent and the passive-aggressive. Who do they remind you of? Adults? Not really. They act more like preschool children or underdeveloped adolescents. That may give you some insight on how to respond to them when (not if) you encounter them.

What do you do with young children? How do you handle them? You set limits; you are consistent in what you say and do; you use natural and logical consequences; you do not overexplain or overtalk; you pay attention when they do something right and ignore their bad behavior for the most part. If you pay too much attention to the unacceptable behavior, you will reinforce it.

You may want to review these approaches in a child-rearing book if you're a bit removed from your child-rearing days.

FOREWARNING

Do not personalize the actions or responses of a person with a personality disorder. Their responses aren't about you. These individuals do not really care about you except for what you can do for them. If you have difficulty saying no and tend to be a people pleaser, you will probably find yourself enmeshed and end up in some convoluted relationships and situations.[8]

There are a few other steps you can take to avoid ending up in close interaction with a personality-disordered person. If you are contemplating hiring a person or teaming up to work with a person, and his or her behavior has raised some flags in your mind, think before you respond and consider the possible outcome of your words or actions. Using a delay tactic to give you time to check out the person's story will keep you out of difficulty. Learn as much as you can about the person. What was the pattern and history at a former place of employment or former church? Is what they told you really the truth?

Sometimes it helps to do the unexpected. If you are predictable, these people know how to use you. If they become upset or angry, do not allow their responses to cause you to respond in the same way. Sometimes it helps not to respond to their upset but to continue to interact as if they weren't behaving in this manner.[9]

It's easy to begin thinking that you can change the types we've been talking about. You won't and you can't. Their insights are limited. Remember, for people to change, they need to know they need to change, and they must want to change. You can continue to pray for them, but you may need to consider limiting your time and/or involvement with them.

Although you may be stuck working with an impossible person, and it would be difficult to change the minimum amount of time you spend in that person's presence—they could be your employer, coworker, partner, fellow church board member, fellow choir member, part of your small fellowship group—you can change your availability and the intensity of your involvement with them.

Notes

1. Les Parrott, *High Maintenance Relationships* (Wheaton, IL: Tyndale House Publishers, 1996), n.p.
2. Alan A. Cavaiola, Ph.D., and Neil J. Lavender, Ph.D, *Toxic Coworkers* (Oakland, CA: New Harbinger Publications, 2000), p. 13.
3. Albert J. Bernstein, Ph.D., *Emotional Vampires* (New York: McGraw Hill, 2000), pp. 139-148, adapted, and Cavaiola and Lavender, *Toxic Coworkers*, pp. 31-34, adapted.
4. Bernstein, *Emotional Vampires*, pp. 33-58, adapted.
5. Derek Kidner, *Proverbs* (Downers Grove, IL: InterVarsity Press, 1964), pp. 40-42.
6. Bernstein, *Emotional Vampires*, pp. 87-97, adapted.
7. Cavaiola and Lavender, *Toxic Coworkers*, pp. 4, 5, adapted.
8. Bernstein, *Emotional Vampires*, p. 14, adapted.
9. Ibid., pp. 77-83; 148-153, adapted.

CHAPTER 4

HOW TO CONTROL
A CONTROLLER

*I used to look forward to serving on my church board. But lately I'd rather
avoid the meetings. Most everyone there has good ideas and likes to contribute,
but there are two people who have to have it their way. No matter what any of
us say or do (including our pastor), these two end up deciding what happens.*

Over the last thirty years I've worked with a multitude of couples
in counseling and in seminars as well as with individuals in businesses and corporations. One of the major people problems
I consistently encounter, whether it emerges in a marriage, family, work or church relationship, is the person who needs to control. Some people feel called not just to control their own lives
but also the lives of those around them.

Take marriage, for example. It is possible for love to die. At
the top of the list of behaviors that kill love is acting in a con-

trolling way. I know this is true because I've seen it happen too many times.

Control tactics can involve a variety of behaviors, including overt acts of disregard toward a spouse's unique personality qualities, opinions, faith, desires, activities or lifestyle. Control can involve forcing one's partner to do something against his or her will and may include criticism, blame and put-downs.

Control shows itself in many forms and disguises. One of the most obvious forms is perfectionism.

CONTROL THROUGH PERFECTIONISM

A wife married for 10 years described her life with a perfectionistic controller:

> Carl is just so critical and particular but not in a loud or angry way. He never raises his voice. But he looks at me, shakes his head or rolls his eyes to show his disgust over what I've done. If not that, I get what I call the "soft lecture." He doesn't raise his voice, get angry or sound firm. Rather, he talks in a soft, patient condescending tone of voice implying, "How could you have been so stupid?" Sometimes I get the silent treatment and some sighs. That's the signal for me to figure out what I've done wrong.
>
> There have even been times, believe it or not, when he has taken the fork out of my mouth because I'm eating too much, turned off the TV because I shouldn't be watching that program, or corrected my volume of talking in public. I'm tired of it. I'm tired of going along with what he's doing. I can't deny who I am and I can't live trying to figure out how to please him.

Besides, I've heard this so much I've begun to doubt myself. I've even thought, "Maybe he's right. Maybe I need to do what he says. Maybe I am creating the problems." But fortunately I came to my senses."[1]

This type of behavior also happens with other relationships, whether at work or at church, and it is just as disruptive to those relationships.

There are many controllers out there. Some are referred to as *control freaks*. You can expect most control freaks to be obnoxious, tenacious, invasive, obsessive, perfectionistic, critical, irritable, demanding, rigid and close-minded. Do you know what the word "obnoxious" means? It comes from the Latin *noxius*, which means hurtful. Many control freaks are just that, hurtful. They injure nearly every relationship they have because of their controlling and destructive ways.[2]

Control freaks display their control tactics in a variety of ways. They may nag, threaten, intimidate or filibuster. They're quite direct in what they do, and the message is quite obvious to all around. Other types of controllers are a bit more subtle and display a unique talent for manipulation. Sometimes their mixed messages and deceptions are so subtle that you don't realize what they are doing until it's been done. A controller is determined to get his or her own way, no matter what the cost to you.

It's not easy to deal with such a person. The interaction can leave you feeling angry, frustrated, resentful or victimized. Put up a brick wall to stop them and they fly through it like Superman. They can see what they're doing to others but that doesn't stop them. They have a need and a drive to control others.[3]

Les Parrott describes controllers like this:

The very act of someone's trying to control you sends several negative messages: I don't trust you to do it right; I don't respect your judgment; I don't think you are competent; I don't value your insight (or skill or experience). Isn't it true? You feel disrespected because the Control Freak seems to assume you know nothing. Control Freaks can rob you of your sense of confidence and self-control.

Just how does this happen? Control Freaks' techniques are numerous: showing false friendliness, giving expensive gifts, making empty promises, sulking, shouting, nagging, being chronically late, withholding affection, bullying, badgering, or just plain bossing the people around them. The tools of the control trade are infinite.[4]

Have you ever found yourself doing something and wondering how you ever agreed to do it in the first place? You're not alone. Controllers are all around us. In fact, you and I are both "controllers" to a certain degree. We all want some type of control in our life. But when we begin to control others around us, we're like a country with a grandiose sense of entitlement that has just invaded a neighboring country.

Controllers either overpower us or they undermine with indirect tactics. In order to render their tactics useless (which can be done) you need to know their strategies.

DIRECT AND INDIRECT CONTROL TACTICS

Attack
Sometimes controllers just take control without asking permission or announcing what they're going to do. They assume they have the right to do what's being done. Other controllers assault you verbally or emotionally with anger, ridicule, criticism or contempt. And yes, I have seen this occur in church situations as well as in the work force. It is really difficult when a husband and wife work together and one responds to the other this way.

Intimidation

Some controllers intimidate. This works if they have a reputation and a set of intimidating moves. Others use reasoning and logic. They overwhelm and control you by their logical arguments and presentations. If you object, they turn up the intensity. To them, feelings have no value whatsoever.

Erosion

One of the most effective approaches a controller uses is erosion. I've seen the effect of the waves of a storm pounding away on the beaches here in Southern California. Again and again and again, hour after hour, the waves hit. In time the beach that many paid hundreds of thousands of dollars for no longer exists. In a similar way, controllers wear you down by their repetitive destructive behavior. Stubborn isn't a strong enough label for their approaches.

> We all want some type of control in our life. But when we begin to control others around us, we're like a country with a grandiose sense of entitlement that has just invaded its neighboring country.

Deception, Guilt and Disconnection

Some tactics a controller uses are more immediate, such as making decisions and arrangements first and then letting others know. Deception tactics such as lies or omissions seem to work well for them also. Then there are the emotional expectation tactics such as inducing guilt, treating you with silence or disconnecting from you.

Do any of these tactics sound familiar to you? Can you think of someone in your workplace who uses these tactics? If so, how did their tactics affect the work environment or the ministry of your church?

Why are controllers successful in being controllers? It's simple. *Others cooperate with them.* They *accommodate* them. Many people accommodate a controller without even being aware of it. When you accommodate, you are allowing the other person's behavior to control your own. What has worked with others to change behavior probably will not work with this person.

For some people, controlling is a way of life; for others, accommodating is a way of life. Controllers go after what they want and accommodators react to what is said or done.

ACCOMMODATORS

How do accommodators respond to the tactics of a controller? Some give in. They yield to keep the peace. How? There are many ways:

- backing down if there's going to be a disagreement
- flattering or second-guessing to keep the controller from getting angry
- placating or appeasing or even doing something underhanded

Many are people pleasers and feel this is the way they must behave as Christians. But people pleasers seem to have weak boundaries that anyone can invade. People pleasers tend to:

- quickly correct whatever a controller objects to
- check with the controller to make sure he or she approves
- make up for the controller's displeasure by doing what the controller wants, and then some

• chase after the controller who withdraws and try to "fix" everything

Do these actions solve the problems created by controlling behavior and build better relationships? No. Some accommodators go further and become self-sacrifices—they say yes to any request, regardless of how much they already have to do. If someone suggests they might hurt or offend someone by a particular request, they give in and pick up the slack for others who seem to be helpless.

Then there are accommodators who fight back. But some never fight back directly. That would be too threatening. They do it in passive ways like tuning out, acting helplessly, asking endless questions, procrastinating or using sarcasm. Some retaliate or outright rebel. Do any of these actions resolve conflicts and build better relationships? No.

DEALING WITH A CONTROLLER

If You Can't Fight 'em, Join 'em
There is one step you *can* take to not only deal with a controller in your life but to get along better and perhaps even build a better relationship.

There are times when your best choice is to go along with what the controller wants. But you are *choosing* to do this. It doesn't mean you're losing or giving in. It means you are making the choice to do so since it seems to be the best possible choice. It may be the beginning of planting the seeds of a give-and-take relationship.[5]

Les Parrott suggests:

By cooperating with Control Freaks' need to be in control, you can help them calm down and be less controlling.

Control Freaks can attempt to control only so much; if they have more confidence in you because you have stayed calm and can work with their input, they may begin to let up on you.

Think of Control Freaks as overprotective parents. One of the best ways to help them relax is to keep them informed. The more information you give, the less they have to worry and the more they'll let go. This strategy is similar to "going with the control."[6]

Standing Your Ground

There are times when the best choice is to be tenacious and stand your ground. The way in which you do this is important. You can be calm, definite and persistent, even if the controller is loud and irate.

It also helps to learn to use the broken record technique. I realize that today, with CDs and cassettes, there are some people who have never seen a vinyl record. Records came in three speeds—78, 45 and 33-1/3 RPM. As the vinyl disk went around on the turntable, the needle would sometimes get stuck in a groove and the same phrase would be repeated again and again. This is where our phrase "broken record" comes from.

When you use the broken record technique, repeating your answer, response or request again and again, regardless of what the other person says, eventually the other person begins to yield. If you keep responding to a request with, "No, I will be unable to do that," you will stay in control.

When you are asked for your reasons (and you will be) just repeat the same statements. You don't have to give your reasons. If you do, you just give the controller more power. The broken record approach does work! In time the controller may develop some respect for you because of your strength.

I've found in counseling that if I'm working with a strong, abrupt, dominant individual, as portrayed in their communication style, and I respond in the same style (I'm mirroring what I see and hear) this person listens to me and respects what I say. He sees strength because I'm speaking his language. (Much more on this subject later).

Disconnecting from the Controller

There are times when your best move may be to disconnect. You don't always have to participate or cooperate with the controller. Getting out of the situation by leaving, by anticipating their moves and eluding, ignoring and not responding are some of the options you have. This would mean leaving the scene, spending less time with the person, not chasing them if they sulk, ignoring barks and not asking for a controller's permission unless necessary.

Honesty Can Be the Best Policy

Another approach is called "leveling." It's simply being honest with the other person. It's an expression of the trait described in Ephesians 4:15: "speaking the truth in love." One author suggests that this means speaking the truth in such a way that your relationship is better than it was before. It entails sharing what you think and feel about what the other person is suggesting. The sole purpose of this approach is to convey information—not to criticize, condemn or change the other person. This can involve letting the controller know what you dislike, what you do like and what you would prefer in the future.[7]

One of the best actions is to ask yourself, What does this person need from me that might lessen his need or desire to control me?[8]

In the act of leveling you are trying to resolve the issue. The same principles we use in resolving conflict, listed below, will help when leveling with a controller.

Speak directly and personally to the other person. Don't assume the controller knows what you are thinking and feeling. If anything, assume that he or she knows very little and this is the first time to deal with the issue. "In the end, people appreciate frankness more than flattery" (Prov. 28:23, *TLB*).

Be honest in your statements and questions. Ephesians 4:15,23 are important verses to practice, both in making statements and in asking questions.

Turn your questions into statements. Too often in a conflict one person feels as if he or she is participating in an inquisition.

Focus on desired or positive changes rather than on faults, defects or what you hope to avoid. This helps the other person become aware of what is gratifying and helpful to you. Believe it or not, it's easier, psychologically speaking, to begin new behaviors than to terminate old behaviors. Don't apologize for your feelings or your needs.

Make "I" statements rather than "you" statements and share your present feelings rather than your past thoughts or feelings.

Select an appropriate time. "A man has joy in making an apt answer, and a word spoken at the right moment—how good it is!" (Prov. 15:23, *AMP*).

Define the problem. How do you define the problem and how does the controller define it? You could suggest that you both stop talking and write down exactly what it is you are trying to resolve.

Define the areas of agreement and disagreement in the conflict.
Share first with the other person what the two of you
agree on, and then ask what he or she disagrees with you
about. Writing the areas of agreement and disagreement
on paper helps to clarify the situation.

Here comes the difficult part. *Identify your own contribution to the problem.* A few conflicts may be one-sided, but
most involve contributions from both sides. When you
accept some responsibility for a problem, the other person sees a willingness to cooperate and will probably be
much more open to the discussion.

The next step is to *state positively what behaviors on your
part would probably help; be willing to ask for his or her
opinion.*

There are numerous statements you can use, such as: "I'm a
bit confused right now about what's been said. Could you start
at the top? I'd like to respond to each point."

If the person is angry, suggest, "I'd like to catch everything
you're saying. Could you say it slower and then I think I could really grasp it." When a person slows down, anger seems to subside.

You may want to document what you say with, "It appears
you're upset at me since your voice was raised and you slammed
the book on the desk. Can you tell me what you want from me
so I can be clear and then consider your request?"

One author suggested using the "when statement"
approach to help the controller become more aware of his or her
behavior:

"When you do (or say) _____ I feel _____" or
"When I do/say _____ you seem to _____."[9]

Do not hesitate to share requests with the person. Some
requests will be simple and some will be complex. Don't apolo-

gize for your request, which will vary but should contain words such as the following:

> "Would you please . . ."
> "It would be helpful if . . ."
> "I'd really appreciate . . ."
> "I'd prefer . . ."

This is simple and basic communication but easy to forget if you're overly intimidated by a controller.

If the controller uses criticism, there are several ways to respond. Contain your defensiveness. A lot of people find it difficult if not impossible to say: "I'm wrong; you may be right." If necessary, practice saying this sentence so that you will be able to say it when the need arises.

Proverbs 28:13 (TLB) has good advice: "A man who refuses to admit his mistakes can never be successful. But if he confesses and forsakes them, he gets another chance."

Sometimes you will have to admit that you are wrong in the face of the controller's criticism, and this is never easy. It also can be tricky. Be sure not to play the "I know it's all my fault" game with them. When you face the criticism and know it's correct, keep these proverbs in mind:

> If you refuse criticism you will end in poverty and disgrace; if you accept criticism you are on the road to fame (Prov. 13:18, TLB).

> Don't refuse to accept criticism; get all the help you can (Prov. 23:12, TLB).

> It is a badge of honor to accept valid criticism (Prov. 25:12, TLB).

If you really are at fault, then be willing to admit it. Say something like, "You know, I do think I'm to blame here. I'm sorry for what I said and I'm sorry that I hurt you. What can I do to help or make up for it?"

I realize this step may be easier said than done. Looking for value in criticism may be like searching for a needle in a haystack. But you must ask yourself, What can I learn from this experience? Is there a grain of truth to which I need to respond? These questions will shift you from the position of the defendant in a relationship to that of an investigator.

However unfair the attack, disregard the negative statements. Give the other person permission to exaggerate. Eventually the exaggerated statements will blow away like chaff and only the truth will remain. Keep searching for the grain of truth and try to identify the real cause for the criticism. Then ask yourself, What is the main point here? What does he (or she) want to happen as a result of our discussion? Remember: If three people call you a horse, it may be time to buy a saddle.

At times, the process of investigating an accusation or criticism may overwhelm you with anger, confusion or frustration. In the rush of these emotions, your mind may pull a disappearing act and go blank. You need time to think before you respond. How can you do that?

First, let me warn you about how *not* to do it. Don't ask, "Can I take a minute to think about this?" You don't need anyone's permission to take time to think. And don't say, "Are you sure you're seeing this situation accurately?" This question gives the controller the opportunity to make another value judgment on the issue and vests him or her with unneeded power.

It's better to say, "I'm going to take a few minutes to think this over." You can also respond with noncommittal statements like, "That's an interesting point" or "That's a possibility" or "I'd not seen it in that way." With these statements you are not being defensive and you are not caving in.

Controllers do not have to control. And just remember, controllers do not have all the power you think they do unless you give it to them.

One last thought: Could it be that the amount of control a person tries to exert is in proportion to the amount of fear they experience about life? It's something to consider.

Notes

1. H. Norman Wright and Dr. Gary Oliver, *How to Bring Out the Best in Your Spouse* (Ann Arbor, MI: Servant Publications, 1994), p. 209.
2. Les Parrott, *The Control Freak* (Wheaton, IL: Tyndale House Publishers, 2000), p. 22, adapted.
3. Gerald W. Piaget, Ph.D., *Control Freaks* (New York: Doubleday, 1991), p. 8, adapted.
4. Parrott, *The Control Freak*, pp. 11, 12.
5. Piaget, *Control Freaks*, pp. 48-60, adapted.
6. Les Parrott, *High Maintenance Relationships* (Wheaton, IL: Tyndale House Publishers, 1996), pp. 84, 85.
7. Piaget, *Control Freaks*, pp. 102-116, adapted.
8. Ibid., p. 147, adapted.
9. Ibid., p. 170.

CHAPTER 5

PEOPLE CAN CHANGE

*Why do people do some of the things they do? It just doesn't make sense. Oh
sure, most people are OK, but some really get to me. One guy seems to have a
calling in life to be a problem. Is there anything I can do to change him? I'd
enjoy my work so much more if only . . .*

By now you know—either from what you've read or by what
you've experienced firsthand—that you will meet impossible
people at work and at church. You'll also meet some mildly irritating people. Sometimes the reason they are irritating is that
they're just a bit different than you, or you don't know how to
communicate and respond in a way that helps them change.
Although we don't do it purposely, sometimes the way we
respond to others actually reinforces their bothersome habits.

Are there any people you would like to change? Sure there
are. It's all right to admit it. You may have some people in your

life who drive you crazy. You just want to be sure you're not help-ing them to stay in this kind of behavior.

Have you ever had a relationship situation at work where you've made a request to another person for a change and it didn't have any effect? You could respond by giving up and seething inside—you know, a little green monster begins to grow inside of you and plots what you'd like to do to this irritant! Or you could continue to try to change the person in the same way you've tried before—only now you intensify your approach. The problem with either approach is that nothing will change. That makes it easy to believe that the other person is stubborn, obsti-nate and unmovable. The reality may be that it's your approach that needs to change. When you use the same unsuccessful approach over and over again, it simply reinforces the likelihood that the offensive behavior will be repeated.

Sometimes I say to those I see in counseling, "If what you're doing isn't working, why keep on doing it? There's got to be a bet-ter way." It's so easy for us to focus on the other person and fail to see our own contribution to the problem. The phrases to use in getting through to another person are, "What could *I* do differ-ently? How could I express this differently?" In other words, are you talking in a way that connects with the other person?

When you are having difficulty with someone, it's helpful to ask yourself, "What is this person doing or saying that presents a problem, and in what way is this a problem?"[1]

CONCENTRATION ON THE WHAT, NOT THE WHY

Sometimes we get stuck in working out a relationship with some-one not so much because of the communication issues but because of our own responses as we attempt to bring about a change. The author of *How to Work With Just About Everyone* believes that one of the reasons we get stuck is that we speculate about *why* another person is a problem rather than describing what the basic problem is. The why can be expressed in several ways.

What Makes Him Do That?

You can concentrate on understanding why another person is responding in a certain way, but if you speculate, you could be way off base. Knowing why usually doesn't change the problem.

Similarly, if you speculate about a person's intentions instead of describing what they do that bothers you, that's like mind reading and leads to not really seeing a situation for what it is. It keeps you from getting the information you need.

The third expression of *why* is to slap a label on the person in place of describing the behavior that bothers you. Instead of saying a person is insensitive, it may help to say she doesn't listen and she interrupts on a continual basis.

The fourth expression of *why* is thinking in terms of right and wrong. It's easy to assign labels, isn't it? If we get caught in this trap we don't have to figure out what the real problem is. If we think we are right, *all* the effort goes into changing the other person and we fail to see our own contribution.

We don't need to know why, we simply need to know what the issue is.[2]

THE SOURCE OF CHANGE

It's simple to get another person to change. I work on this all the time with couples in marriage counseling. If you want someone to change, change yourself. The same principle is true for all troubled relationships.

Charles made an appointment for counseling and was right on time for his first session. "Norm," he said, "I'm here because I have a few people at my place of business who are very difficult to get along with. They are problem people—which I refer to as PPs—and we're devoting far too much time to them in our office. If we could just get them to change their behavior and not be so much of a problem to everyone, our production would increase and we would eliminate a lot of difficulties in the office."

It's simple to get another person to change—change yourself. The same principle is true for all troubled relationships.

After listening to Charles vividly describe his problem for about five minutes, I said, "Charles, are you also saying that you have difficulty getting along with some of these people?"

"At times it's difficult for me," he admitted. "But some of my coworkers have a much greater problem dealing with them than I do. And some of my friends at work need some help in learning how to deal with the PPs. But my main reason for coming to see you is for you to help me figure out a way to change these PPs. I'm sure there must be a way."

Does Charles's problem sound familiar? At times we've all thought, *If only so-and-so would change, everything would be so much better!*

"Charles," I replied, "there are three possible ways to resolve this problem. If it's okay with you, I would like to explore all three of those ways with you. One way to rid your company of problem people is to change the environment. In this instance, it may involve transferring those people to another office or division. If they are a serious problem, you might consider replacing them. What do you think of this option?"

Charles responded immediately by saying, "I don't think that would work. There are too many problems and unpleasant consequences with reassigning people. Give me another option."

"Have you ever tried to change the way the problem people are themselves—the way they respond at work? Have you talked to them, made suggestions, considered options, encouraged them, complimented them, affirmed them?"

Charles interrupted me. "Norm, I think I've tried everything you've suggested. Perhaps I haven't done very much with compliments and encouragement. When the PPs create so many problems, it's difficult to do that. No, the direct approach hasn't worked very well. I'm hoping that you have another sure-fire tactic or method that will do the trick."

I paused for a moment and then said, "There is one other possibility. This approach has always had the best results." I looked at Charles, waiting to see if he could figure it out first.

Suddenly Charles gave me a pained look. "Oh no, Norm! You're not going to suggest that old line, 'If you want someone to change, start by changing yourself,' are you?"

"Do you have a better idea, Charles? You said that what you've already tried hasn't worked. This is the best solution I have ever found."

Charles's reply was characteristic of how many people feel about making changes in their own lives. He said, "I don't think it's fair that I have to change. After all, the PPs are the problem. Why shouldn't they change?"

"That may be true, Charles," I said, shaking my head in agreement. "But can you suggest another way to change them?"

He was thoughtfully silent for a moment. Then he said, "What should I change and how should I go about it? It's not easy, you know. These people do and say things that really push my buttons. I just want to put them in their place and get on with life."

"What you're telling me, Charles, is that you allow the problem people to control you. You're saying that when they do or say certain things, you can't control yourself. How long have these people had this much control over you?"

Charles's face looked pale from shock. He almost shouted out his response. "You're right! I've been so dumb! I never saw it before! I've been letting them determine how I act. To be honest, I'm not real proud of how I've acted sometimes. I've let them push my buttons and blamed them for the trouble that resulted. I guess I've really cooperated with them, haven't I?"

We often allow others to get to us without seeing how we cooperate with them through our reactions.

BEHAVIOR THAT NEEDS A NEW RESPONSE

Silence

Let's consider some common problems that impede good communication. The silent partner in communication is the one who often won't respond. This could be because he or she doesn't know what to say at the time, is afraid of the other's response, just doesn't want to talk or is using silence as a control issue. These responses drive the partner who wants to talk up the wall. To get the silent partner to respond, what does the other partner do? He or she puts even more pressure on a response or even makes threats. Does it work? Not on your life. You may know someone like this at work and it can be quite frustrating when you're looking for their contribution.

Disruption

Perhaps you know people at work who are disruptive in some way—interrupting, making smart comments or even using sarcasm to comment about what others have said or done. Will asking them to stop change their responses? Not usually.

Procrastination

What do you do when someone is consistently late to work or with some of their projects? Their work is really good and you don't want them to leave, but the lateness is a problem. You know they are late and they know it; you've talked about it, but nothing has changed.

Inattention

Is there a person at work who doesn't listen to what you say? Most of us know individuals like this. Perhaps you've asked them to listen to you or confronted them about their poor listening habits. Has this brought about a lasting change? Probably not.

RESPONSES THAT DON'T WORK

There are several ineffective ways to try to solve people problems at work. Some of the difficulties are like a splinter in your finger; they don't cause disability, but they sure do irritate. Your difficult person could be someone who gossips, complains, uses sarcasm or takes up too much of your time, etc.

Sometimes we think it's easier not to confront the issue directly. Most of us would like to avoid conflict. We think, "If I don't say anything, the problem will go away." If that doesn't work, then we try the indirect means. We imply what we'd like them to change and then hope it works. There are many ways to do this. You could hint, joke, use nonverbals like rolling your eyes or folding your arms and sighing, or use sarcasm. Most people either ignore hints or just don't get them. So you end up feeling an even greater sense of frustration.

Another approach that seems safe is the lob. It's like a shotgun blast at several targets. You hope to hit the right target—except this doesn't work. Here are some classic lobs:

"It seems as though some in our office aren't following the necessary procedures."

"We all need to put forth an effort to be here on time for this week's meeting."

"We all need to be sure to keep the lounge clean and pick up after ourselves."

The culprits usually fail to recognize that the message is for them.

General suggestions won't work either. When you suggest that a person "Shape up," "Get your act together," "Be more productive or more professional," or "Be sure to check in with me" what do these statements mean? They won't correct anything. Most people do not read between the lines. You need to be specific.[3]

All it takes is a small change on your part to experience some major long-lasting effects. An example of this principle comes from the meteorologist, Edward Larenz. His task was to analyze the effects a small change would have on global weather patterns. He was able to determine that changes so small that you wouldn't consider them significant have a profound impact on systems like our weather. He described what he learned as the "Butterfly Effect," since a butterfly flapping its wings in Brazil might create a tornado in Texas. The same is true in relationships. Small but significant changes can help people improve the way they get along.[4]

THE 180-DEGREE TURNAROUND

Every one of these behavior problems is changeable. How? I've mentioned the first step already—change the way you respond to the behavior. How? Do the opposite. Don't tell the person to change. Tell him *not to change.* Do a complete 180-degree turnaround.

Many sports enthusiasts will remember the high jumper Dick Fosbury. He was doing just all right in the high jump, but he wasn't satisfied. He decided that he needed to do something different. So instead of running up to the high bar and rolling over it facedown, he turned and arched his back, launching himself over the bar belly up and kicking his legs up and over last. People were shocked and then they laughed. That is until he won a Gold Medal in the 1968 games with a seven-foot, four-and-a-half inch jump. Most high jumpers today do the "Fosbury Flop." His solution was a complete turnaround—a 180-degree switch.[5]

How do you begin to do that?

First, *write down what you see as the problem*—state it simply and factually.

Next, *identify what you have been doing and the results* in terms of both changes in the behavior and the effect it has had on your relationship.

Then, (gulp), *do a complete 180 degree.*

If you begin doing the opposite of what you've been doing, it takes a leap of faith. In a sense you're telling the other person *not* to change. It sort of sounds like reverse psychology, doesn't it? Like telling your child *not* to eat all her beets and because you said that she eats them. In a sense, that's what I'm saying.

Part of your concern will probably be that it won't work and could get worse. That's always a possibility, but if you continue to do what you're doing now, it won't work either.

Finally, when the other person does change, *maintain this new plan.* Don't revert back to your old habits.[6]

EFFECTIVE RESPONSES THAT BRING ABOUT CHANGE

Breaking Their Silence

Let's go back to the earlier examples. Remember the silent person? How can you respond in the opposite way? Many have used the approach of making statements such as, "I appreciate that you don't always respond or chime in since it gives me time to sort things through out loud or by myself. I know you'll say something when you've had a chance to think it through," or "We appreciate that you quietly think things through in the meeting since it gives the rest of us an opportunity to say more," or "Here's something I'd like you to think about for a while and we can discuss it at a later time. In fact, it would be best if we didn't talk about it now. Here's what I was thinking . . ." (Quite often this last statement causes the person to want to discuss the issue right then and there.)

Responding to Disruption

You can respond to those who disrupt with, "I've noticed that when you make your remarks there's usually some good points that cause us to reconsider what we've come up with. And it seems like our boss likes what I do when I listen to your comments, so keep on with them. They're helpful."[7]

Dealing with Lateness

When talking with a person who is chronically late, you could say, "I like your flexible approach to your work. It's helping the rest of us to view our jobs in a bit more relaxed way. Since some of us are here earlier and have already put our heads together and planned for the day, we'll leave a note on your desk of what we need from you or you can check with your supervisor, Jim, so he's aware that you need to be brought up to speed." (This also involves some consequences.)

Listen Up!

When someone isn't listening, be sure to package what you say in that person's learning and language style. Sometimes a person starts out listening to you but because of personality preference (intuitives especially) their minds can take off down another bunny trail simply because of something you say.

Here are a couple of ways to keep their attention: "I need just 87 seconds of your time since this is so important. On a scale of 0-10, it's a 12" or "What I have to say isn't that important, so you don't have to listen with both ears."

You could also throw in a wild statement every now and then like, "I'm going to Tahiti next week on company expense." When you get a shocked response, say, "I was just checking to see if you were listening." Or whenever you talk with this individual, ask him or her to summarize what you've said: "I just want to make sure you've heard what I said so we're on the same page. Could you give me a summation of what I went over with you?" If you do this each and every time, this person should learn to pay attention and give you accurate feedback.

THE FRUIT OF GOOD COMMUNICATION

Although you may think it's easier to avoid some of these issues we've discussed, I like what Lucy Gill said: "When you avoid the problem, you avoid the solution."[8]

If you plan in advance what you would like to say and even rehearse it, you will feel a greater comfort level when you talk to a coworker about a concern. Don't focus on the problem; point to the desired behavior. When you talk about what you would like to see happen, the person is more likely to remember it. If you point to the offensive behavior by saying, "You're wasting time" or "I don't like to hear your complaints" or "I wish you would keep your work station cleaner," you will only reinforce the offending behavior. Instead say:

"I really appreciate it when you're aware of the time constraints we're working under. It helps all of us."

"I really appreciate it when you give positive suggestions as well as notice what's working around here."

"It really helps all of us here when you keep your area cleaned up like you've done in the past."

When a person responds in the way you like, reinforce that behavior with a thank-you or a compliment. You'll see a difference.

It may be helpful to consider the times when you're getting along quite well with those at work. What is the difference about these times compared with the times of difficulty? Usually we focus more on what the other person is doing differently, but it may help more to determine what we might be doing differently. Once again, focus more on yourself than on the other person.

Here's a different thought: If there are conflicts at work, why not spend some time determining what makes them end? Most of the people I see in counseling want to talk about how arguments start. This isn't very productive. We've found it is better to talk about how they end. When you can figure out what makes you call a truce, you can make some choices the next time to short-circuit the progression of the disagreement.[9]

Remember, changing yourself works better than trying to change others. And even if you see no changes in other people, your own changes will make life better for you and will reflect God's Word and power in your life. When you do change, your bad relationships can turn to good relationships, and your good relationships can get even better.

Notes

1. Lucy Gill, *How to Work with Just About Everyone* (New York: A Fireside Book, Simon and Schuster, 1999), p. 49, adapted.
2. Ibid., pp. 62-67, adapted.
3. Ibid., p. 142, adapted.
4. Michele Werner-Davis, *Divorce Busting* (New York: A Fireside Book, Simon and Schuster, 1992), pp. 160-163, adapted.
5. Gill, *How to Work with Just About Anyone*, pp. 120-124, adapted.
6. Werner-Davis, *Divorce Busting*, p. 92, adapted.
7. Gill, *How to Work with Just About Anyone*, p. 102, adapted.
8. Ibid., p. 127.
9. Werner-Davis, *Divorce Busting*, p. 136, adapted.

CHAPTER 6

THOSE WHO LISTEN GET ALONG BEST

Sometimes I wonder if it's me or the other person that's different. We've got some real talkers in the group. In fact, I think some need to go to one of those talker's recovery groups called On & On.

Whether you're at work or at church you hear a lot of talking going on, but is anybody listening? That's questionable when so many people have their own agendas. If there is no true listening going on, then there is no communication, no relationship and no getting along.

One of the greatest gifts one person can give another is the gift of listening. It is an act of connection and caring. But far too many only hear themselves talking. Few listen. Often when two people are talking they are having, for the most part, "dialogues of the deaf." The people are talking at one another. But if you truly listen to another person, you are sending a message that will make him think *I must be worth hearing.* If you ignore the person, he will think *I must be dull and boring.*

Have you had the experience of being listened to? Not just heard, but really listened to? Read these verses from the Word of God that speak of how God listens to us:

> The eyes of the LORD are toward the righteous, and His ears are open to their cry. The face of the LORD is against evil-doers, to cut off the memory of them from the earth. The righteous cry and the LORD hears, and delivers them out of all their troubles. The LORD is near to the brokenhearted, and saves those who are crushed in spirit (Ps. 34:15-18).

> I love the LORD, because He hears my voice and my sup-plications. Because He has inclined His ear to me, there-fore I shall call upon Him as long as I live (Ps. 116:1,2).

The importance of our listening is also stressed in Scripture:

> Anyone who answers without listening is foolish and confused (Prov. 18:13, *NCV*)

> Any story sounds true until someone tells the other side and sets the record straight (Prov. 18:17, *TLB*).

> The wise man learns by listening; the simpleton can learn only by seeing scorners punished (Prov. 21:11, *TLB*).

> Let every man be quick to hear [a ready listener] (Jas. 1:19, *AMP*).

Who would you say really listens to you at work? Whom do you really listen to at work? Who is the best listener you know at church?

What do I mean by listening? What do I mean by hearing? Is there a difference?

Hearing is basically to gain content or information for your own purposes. Listening entails caring for and being empathic toward the person who is talking.

Hearing means that you are concerned about what is going on inside *you* during the conversation. Listening means that you are trying to understand the feelings of *the other person* and are listening for his or her sake.

Let me give you a threefold definition of what it means to listen when another person is talking:

1. You are not thinking about what you are going to say when the other person stops talking. You're not busy formulating your response. You are concentrating on what is being said and you're putting into practice Proverbs 18:13: "He who gives an answer before he hears, It is folly and shame to him."

2. You are completely accepting of what is being said without judging what the person is saying or how he or she says it. You may fail to hear the message if you're thinking that you don't like the tone of voice or the words the person is using. You may react on the spot to the tone and content and miss the meaning. Perhaps the person hasn't said it in the best way, but why not listen and then come back later when both of you are calm and can discuss the proper wording and tone of voice? Acceptance does not mean you have to agree with the content of what is said. Rather, it means that you understand what the person is saying and that it is something he or she feels.

3. You should be able to repeat what the person has said and what you think he or she was feeling while speaking to you. Real listening implies an obvious interest

in a person's feelings and opinions and an attempt to understand the issue from his or her perspective.

"Listening is a sharp attention to what is going on. Listening is an active openness toward your employer or customer. Listening is putting your whole self in a position to respond to whatever your employee cares to say."[1] Listening to your coworker means letting go of your concerns, your wants and your investment in your own position long enough to consider the other person. When you are doing the talking, you're usually not learning. But when you listen, you learn.

Listening is a skill that can be learned. Your mind and ears can be taught to hear more clearly. And your eyes can be taught to see more clearly. But the reverse is also true. You can learn to *hear* with your *eyes* and *see* with your *ears*. Jesus said:

Therefore I speak to them in parables; because while seeing they *do not see*, and while hearing they *do not hear*, nor do they understand. And in their case the prophecy of Isaiah is being fulfilled, which says, "You will keep on hearing, but you will not understand; and you will keep on seeing, but will not perceive; for the heart of this people has become dull, and with their ears they scarcely hear, and they have closed their eyes lest they should see with their eyes, and hear with their ears, and understand with their heart and return, and I should heal them" (Matt. 13:13-15, italics mine).

At work and at church, let your ears hear and see and let your eyes see and hear. You'll be amazed at what's being said that no one is hearing.

The word "hear" in the New Testament does not usually refer to an auditory experience. It usually means to pay heed. As you listen to those around you, you need to pay heed to what is being said. It means tuning into the right frequency.

> If you listen you adventure in the lives of other people. We soon notice the people who really take us seriously and listen to what we have to say. And with them we tend to open more of our lives than with the busy nonlistener. We share what really matters. Thus, if you are such a listener, the chances are good that others will invite you as a guest into their lives. Because they know you will hear them, they will entrust you with things that mean very much to them. And this too is more rewarding![2]

My retarded son, Matthew, did not have a vocabulary. I learned to listen to him with my eyes. I could read the message in his nonverbal signals. Because of Matthew, I learned to listen to others in the same way and came to understand what my counselees could not put into words. I learned to listen to the message behind the message—the hurt, the ache, the frustration, the loss of hope, the fear of rejection, the feeling of betrayal, the joy, the delight, the promise of change.

Now when I listen to those I counsel, I reflect upon what I see on their faces, in their posture, walk and pace, and I tell them what I see. This gives them an opportunity to explain further what they are thinking and feeling. They *know* I'm tuned in to them.

THE MOST INFLUENTIAL COMPONENTS OF COMMUNICATION

Were you aware that every message has three components? They are the actual content, the tone of voice and the nonverbal communication. But it is the last two components—tone of voice and nonverbal expression—that give the content meaning. It is possible to express many different messages when using the same word, statement, or question simply by changing tone of voice or body movement. Nonverbal communication includes facial expression, body posture and actions.

All components of communication must be complementary in order for a simple message to be transmitted correctly. All the same, we tend to look for nonverbal clues to fully understand what someone is saying. In fact, there is a consensus in research that we generally give a greater percentage weight to the nonverbal component of communication than to the actual content of a message or even to tone of voice.

Tone of Voice

We are usually aware of our content, but not nearly as aware of our tone of voice. You have the capability of giving the same sentence a dozen different meanings, just by changing your tone. Tape record some of your dinner conversations sometime, and then sit down and listen to yourself. You'll be amazed at what you hear.

When it comes to tone of voice or variation of tone, men do not open their jaws as wide as women, so they tend to sound more nasal and monotonal. Actually, men use only three vocal tones, whereas women use more than five. So men tend to use a more staccato (choppy) tone that can come across as abrupt and perhaps less approachable, at least to a woman. Women tend to use more flowing tones when speaking. And a woman will tend to use vocal inflection to emphasize a point, whereas a man uses loudness.[3]

There's an old saying among preachers: When a point in your sermon is weak, raise your voice. I've heard hundreds of different speakers over the past 45 years. Some were loud, some weren't. The loud ones (yellers or shouters) didn't have that much impact on me. But I really heard those who made their point by changes in tone of voice and through pauses.

Listen to others' tone of voice. Listen to your own. Tape record some conversations. Listen to how some speakers use tone of voice. In raising and training both Shelties and Golden Retrievers, I've found that it's the tone of voice that makes the difference. The right tone can cause them to come running to me, stop or stay in place for several minutes. It's not loudness that makes a difference, it's tone.

Often in a phone conversation you don't say you need to terminate the conversation or that you are finished. You use a change in tonal quality to accomplish this. One of my Shelties taught this to me years ago. It seemed as though Prince had this unique ability to know when I was concluding a phone conversation, for he would show up during the last 10 seconds of the conversation with a tennis ball in his mouth. It was as though he was saying, "I know you're about through. It's time to play ball." I soon discovered that he had figured out the change in my voice.

We often send confusing messages because the three components of sending a message contradict each other. When an employer says to his employee, "You did a good job," with the proper tone of voice but with his head buried in the paper on his desk, what's the employee to believe? When your coworker asks, "How was your day?" in a flat tone while passing you on the way to another room, what do you respond to, the verbal or nonverbal message? What if you said, "It was lousy. I was depressed and threw up twice." Your coworker would probably say, "Fine," and keep on walking. There's no real listening going on here.

The Function of Nonverbals
Nonverbal expression serves a number of important functions. It's a way of communicating interpersonal attitudes—how much a person likes another person or likes what the person is saying. It can also reveal how a person perceives his or her status in a group of people.

Most relationship problems may grow out of unsatisfactory nonverbal communications. Vocal variables are important carriers of meaning. We interpret the sound of a voice, both consciously and subconsciously. We usually can tell the emotional meanings of the speaker by voice pitch, rate of speech, loudness, and voice quality. We can tell the sincerity or insincerity, the conviction or lack of conviction, the truth or falsity of most statements we hear. When a voice is raised in volume and pitch, the words will not convey the same meaning as when spoken softly in a lower register. The high, loud voice, with rapid rate and harsh quality, will likely communicate a degree of emotion that will greatly obscure the verbal message. The nonverbal manner in which a message is delivered is registered most readily by the listener. It may or may not be remembered for recall. However, the communicator tends to recall what he said rather than the manner of his speech.[4]

Nonverbal communication greatly affects how well we get along with others and continually sends them messages about how we perceive their significance.

Nonverbal communication greatly affects how well we get along with others and continually sends them messages about how we perceive their significance. For example, if you are engaged in listening to someone, don't answer the phone or allow yourself to be interrupted. One of the worst (and rudest) interrupters is the call waiting system on phones. If you're talking to someone and you hear the click and then the person you're talking with says, "Hold on a minute, I'll see who it is," how do you feel at that time? Not very important when a clicking sound takes precedence over your conversation. If you have call waiting, let them wait or call back or leave a message.

When you're in conversation, don't let your eyes wander. If you do not have eye contact, you miss out. And remember this fact: Most people tend to repeat what they've said when they don't have eye contact with you since they're not sure you have heard them. That can waste time for both of you.

Nonverbal expression is a revealer of the emotion behind the actual words we express and is one of the best ways of elaborating and exaggerating a point.

It is used as a ritual for saying hello, good-bye and congratulations. Your nonverbals, such as a tender touch, can be used when words are inadequate.

Nonverbal communication is also used to give some emotion to a conversation without interrupting the flow of your words. It can give words a greater impact.[5]

THE VALUE OF AUTHENTIC LISTENING

There are many types of listening. Some people listen for facts, information and details for their own use. Others listen because they feel sorry for the person; they feel a sense of pity. Some people listen to gossip because they get a kick out of the juicy story of another person's failures or difficulties.

There are occasions when people listen out of obligation, necessity or to be polite. They feel stuck. Some who listen are nothing more than voyeurs who have an incessant need to pry and probe into other people's lives. Why do you listen? What are your motives? Any or all of the above? Listening that springs from caring builds closeness, reflects love and is an act of grace.

Sensitive listening and hearing facilitate getting along with one another. Yet far too often the potential for listening lies untapped within us like unmined gold because the mine shaft leading to the rich vein of ore is caved in. All of us have barriers that inhibit our listening. Some barriers are simple and others complex.

Did you know that when you listen you have more influence than when you are talking? Are you aware that the listener, not the speaker, controls the conversation? Probably not, since most of us operate under the myth that the more we talk, the more we influence the listener. If both people in a conversation believe this, the talking escalates and becomes more intense, which is quite sad, because the words fly through the air with nowhere to land. Deafness prevails!

What do I mean by the statement that the listener controls the conversation? Compare the listener to the driver of a car. The one who is talking is like the engine. The engine provides the power, but the person at the wheel has the power to decide where the car will go. You, the listener, can give direction and guide the flow of the conversation by the statements you make and the questions you ask. The more information you receive, the more you have to work with, and this happens by listening.

> Did you know that when you listen you have more influence than when you are talking?

Remember our definition of listening? You should be able to repeat what the person has said and what you think he or she was feeling while speaking to you. Real listening implies an obvious interest in the person's feelings and opinions and an attempt to understand from his or her perspective.

When you can repeat what the person has said with a sense of understanding, this is called *paraphrasing*. It reinforces the person's words so that he or she will continue to talk. When you verbally agree with the talker, you cause the person to share even more.

James Lynch, co-director of the Psycho-Physiological Clinic and Laboratories of the University of Maryland has researched what happens when people pay attention to others through listening. He discovered that genuine healing of the cardiovascular system takes place when you listen to another person. Studies showed that blood pressure rises when people speak, but lowers when they listen.[6]

One other thought about the listener. Some people say, "When I listen, it seems to cause the other person to just talk and talk and talk. Why is that?" Perhaps initially it does, but if you remain perfectly silent, you create such tension within the person speaking that the he or she begins to back off. By not responding, you let the other individual know that you are through with your part of the conversation. I'm not advocating use of the silent treatment here; that is an unfair weapon and will, in time, erode a relationship.

So why listen to other people? The obvious answer is that we've been taught to listen, told to listen and admonished to listen. But there are four basic reasons why we listen to other people.

1. to understand the other person
2. to enjoy the other person
3. to learn something from the one talking (such as learning his or her language)
4. to give help, assistance or comfort to the person

The world is made up of many pseudolisteners who masquerade as the real product. But anyone who has not listened for the above reasons does not *really* listen.

BARRIERS TO LISTENING

In order for caring listening to occur, we need to be aware of some of the common obstacles to this side of communication.

Defensiveness

A defensive response means that we are busy thinking up a rebuttal, an excuse or an exception to what someone is saying. In doing this we miss the message. There are a variety of defensive responses. Perhaps *we reach a premature conclusion.* "All right, I know just what you're going to say. We've been through this before and it's the same old thing."

We may read into the person's words *our own expectations* or *project what we would say in the same situation.*

This response, as well as other defensive postures, is not what Scripture is calling us to do as a listener. "Anyone who answers without listening is foolish and confused" (Prov. 18:13, NCV).

Responding to Explosive Words

Explosive words hook you into a negative defensive response. They create an inner explosion of emotions. Explosive comments include "That's crude"; "That's just like a *woman* (or man)"; "You're *always* late"; You *never* ask me what I think"; "I've been working here longer than you!"; "You're becoming just like the previous person on this job." Not only do we react to explosive words, but we may also consciously choose to use some words that make it difficult for another to listen. What are the explosive words that set you off? What is your coworker's list of explosive words? Certain selected words can cut and wound.

Not all defensiveness is expressed. Outwardly we could be agreeing, but inside we're saying just the opposite. If your boss or a coworker confronts you about a behavior or attitude that is creating a problem, do you accept the criticism or do you defend yourself?

Personal Biases and Attitudes

We may hold unfounded biases toward certain individuals. These could include people who speak in a certain tone of voice, who come from particular ethnic groups, who are of the opposite sex, people who remind us of someone from our past, etc. Because of our biases we reject the person or the personality without listening to what the person has to say. In effect we are saying, "If you're____ (and I don't like people who are ____) I don't need to listen to you." Can you think of any bias that gets in the way of your listening?

Our personal biases will affect how we listen more than we realize. For example, it may be easier for us to listen to an angry person than a sarcastic person; some tones or phrases may be more enjoyable to listen to than others; we can be bothered by repetitive phrases someone uses (and may be unaware of); excessive gestures, such as talking with the hands or waving the arms, can be a distraction. Does anyone come to mind as you read these descriptions?

We may listen more or less attentively to someone who is in a position over us, under us or in a prestigious position. Or if someone is trying to control us, listening may be long gone.

We may assign stereotypes to other people, and this influences the way we listen to them.

One person hears with optimism and another with pessimism. I hear the bad news and you hear the good news. If a coworker shares a frustration and difficult situation with you, you may not hear him because you don't like complaining; it bothers you. Or you may hear him as a person who trusts you enough to share.

Conflicting Listening Styles

Some people are distracted in their listening because of the gender of the person who is speaking. Our expectations of what a man shares and doesn't share and what a woman should not share will influence the way we listen.

Lack of understanding of gender differences in listening and conversation creates problems. Women use more verbal responses to encourage response from the one they're talking to. They're more likely than men to use listening signals like "mm-hmmm" and "yeah" to indicate they are listening. But a man will use this response only when he's agreeing with what a woman is saying. A woman will use it simply to indicate she's listening. You can see the outcome of this misunderstanding!

A man interprets a woman's listening responses as signs that she agrees with him. In his mind he's thinking, *That's good! We can move ahead on that new project.* But later on, he may get irritated when he discovers she wasn't agreeing with him at all. He doesn't realize she was simply indicating her interest in what he was saying and was trying to keep the exchange going. This happens repeatedly in the workplace.

On the other hand, a woman may feel ignored and disappointed because a man doesn't make these listening responses. And then she interprets his quietness as *He doesn't care* or *He's not listening. He's just tolerating me!*

A man is more likely than a woman to make comments throughout the conversation instead of waiting for the other person to finish talking. Women seem to be more bothered than men after they've been interrupted or have not been given any listening feedback. This is why many women complain, "The men at work always interrupt me" or "My boss never listens to me. He always has something to say." Women also use the pronouns "you" and "we" more often to acknowledge the other person. This is good, for these words promote a sense of unity.

With all of these differences, given the contrast between listening and talking styles among men and women, it's easy to see why misunderstandings arise. A woman might easily perceive a man as uninterested or unresponsive. That may not be the case.

It's just his way of responding to everyone, not just to her. If a woman says, "He never listens to me" or "He disagrees with everything I say," it's more a reflection of his communication style than proof of insensitivity.

A woman can avoid misunderstanding by keeping in mind the following tendencies about a man's communication style.

- A man is more likely to interrupt a speaker, whether the speaker is a male or female.
- A man is less likely to respond to the comments of the other person and frequently he makes no response at all, tends to give a delayed response at the end of the other person's statement or shows a minimum degree of enthusiasm.
- A man tends to make more statements of fact or opinion than do women.

Knowing about these differences and accepting them can help you accept the other's style without being offended. This is one of the first steps of what we call *genderflex*, which is understanding the differences, and making it a point to adapt and even use the other gender's style in order to bridge them. (This concept will be expanded in the chapter on gender differences.)[7]

Inner Struggles

We have difficulty listening when our emotional involvement reaches the point where we are unable to separate ourselves from the other person. You may find it easier to listen to the problems of people outside the home rather than those of your own family members. With family you are hindered by your emotional involvement, and listening may also be difficult if you blame yourself for the other person's difficulties.

Hearing what someone else is saying may bring to the surface feelings about similar problems we are facing. Our listening may be hindered if we're afraid that our emotions may be activated. A man may feel very ill at ease as his emotions surge to the surface. Can you think of a time when you felt so overwhelmed with feelings that you were unable to hear what someone was saying?

If a person has certain expectations of you, you may be hindered in listening to that person. If you dislike the other person, you probably won't listen very well. When people speak too loudly or softly you may struggle to keep listening.

You *can* overcome obstacles to listening. The initial step is to identify the obstacle. Of those listed, which obstacle do you identify as yours? Who controls this barrier, you or the one speaking? Perhaps you can rearrange the situation or the conditions so that listening would be easier for you. Have you ever thought of discussing this at work or with the people you work beside at church? You may want to discuss what each of you can do to become better listeners and what you can do to make it easier for others to listen to you.

Interruption

You may be in the habit of interrupting because you feel the other person is not getting to the point fast enough. Or you may be thinking ahead, so you ask for information that would be forthcoming anyway. One thing the person says may make your mind race ahead and you blurt out, "Hold it. I've got a dozen ideas cooking because of what you said. Let me tell you some of them . . ."

It's easy for our minds to wander, for we think at five times the rate we can speak. If a person speaks at the rate of 100 words per minute and you listen at the rate of 500 words per minute, do you put your mind on hold or daydream the rest of the time? Although we process information faster than it can be verbalized, we can choose to stay in pace with the speaker.

Sometimes men and women feel interrupted by the other because of the differences in what they are trying to accomplish with their words. Remember, not all interrupting is interrupting. Some cultural groups don't use many pauses between turns in conversation, since overlapping is just part of their conversational culture. Silence is seen as a lack of rapport. Overlapping another person's comments is a way to keep conversation going.

Some people use pauses; others don't. Some are slow-paced and some are fast. Where you are from in this country will affect the way you speak. People from California expect shorter pauses than those from the Midwest or New England. People from New York expect even shorter pauses. A person from California may appear to be an interrupter based on the speech pattern of someone from the Midwest. But someone from New York may appear to a Californian to be an interrupter.[8]

Overload

Perhaps you have used up all the space available in your mind for information. Someone else comes along with a new piece of information and you feel you just can't handle it. You feel as though you are being bombarded from all sides and you don't have enough time to digest it all. Thus it becomes difficult to listen to anything. Your mind feels like a juggler with too many items to juggle.

Bad Timing

Have you ever heard comments like "Talk? Now? At 8:30 in the morning? I just got to work" or "Just a minute. There's only one more page to read" or "I'd like to listen but I'm already late for an appointment"?

Do you realize there are times when listening isn't appropriate and it's perfectly all right to let another person know? It's all right to postpone listening to someone when you've already listened to another person, when you're under pressure for an immediate deadline or when you have to put out a brush fire—a crisis.

But don't postpone by ignoring. Look at the other person and let her know both that you want to hear what she has to say and when you'll be available to hear it. Continue what you were doing and then make sure you follow through with your commitment to listen at a later date.

Physical Exhaustion

Both mental and physical fatigue make it difficult to listen. There are times when you need to let others know that this isn't a good time, but tell the person when you *will* be able to listen.

Selective Attention

Sometimes we screen the information we hear. This is called *filtered listening*. If we have a negative attitude, we may ignore, distort, or reject positive messages. Often we hear what we want to hear or what fits in with our mindset. If we engage in selective listening we probably engage in selective retention. That means we remember certain comments and situations and forget those we reject.

OVERCOMING BARRIERS TO LISTENING

Go back through the 10 barriers to listening. Which 3 obstacles could you work on this week? How can you become a better listener? Here are a few suggestions.

Understand what you feel about the person speaking. How you view another person affects how you listen to him. The communication of the people around you is colored by how you view them. This view may have been shaped by your observations of the person's past performance or by your own defensiveness.

Listen with your ears, your eyes and your body. If someone says, "Are you listening to me?" and you say yes while walking away or fixating on the computer screen, perhaps you aren't really listening. Concentrate on the person and the message, giving your undivided attention. Turn off the computer or phone when there is an important matter to talk about; set aside what you are doing and listen.

Have you ever had a conversation with someone who never seemed to pause even to take a breath? I've heard many a sermon that could have been so much more effective if only the speaker had learned to pause now and then for emphasis.

Have you ever listened to the pauses in your own speech pattern? Are there any? How long are they? A one-second pause is not really a pause, it's more like taking a breath. When you do pause, be sure to keep eye contact. If you don't, the person may think you've stopped talking and jump in with what he wants to say. If you need to think just a bit, just hold up a finger and say, "I'm thinking for just a few seconds." Most people will get the message. If you learn to pause, others will see you as a person who listens, and you won't feel as pressured to talk since you have more time to think of what you want to say.

After the other person has finished talking, pause to indicate that you weren't just waiting in the wings for your grand entrance. After you've been asked a complicated or serious question, pause. This is for your benefit to give you time to think.

If you feel an argument or disagreement beginning to develop, pause and slow down. The person who slows the interchange actually stays more in control of both the interchange as well as the outcome. You also avoid the problem of making reactionary remarks. You're less likely to be set off by the other person's comments.[9]

Be patient, especially if the other person is a slow or hesitant talker. What if the person is from another country and hasn't yet mastered the English language? If this irritates you, you may have a tendency to jump in whenever you can find an opening, finish the person's sentences or hurry him along. But you can't assume you really know what is going to be said.

If you've been playing the role of a mind reader, consider these ten commandments for better listening:

I. *On passing judgment*. Thou shalt neither judge nor evaluate until thou hast truly understood. "Hold it right there, I've heard enough to know where you stand, and you're all wet."

II. *On adding insights*. Thou shalt not attribute ideas or contribute insights to those stated. "If you mean this, it will lead there, and then you must also mean that."

III. *On assuming agreement*. Thou shalt not assume that what you heard is what was truly said or meant. "No matter what you say now, I heard you with my own ears."

IV. *On drifting attention*. Thou shalt not permit thy thoughts to stray or thy attention to wander. "When you said that, it triggered an interesting idea that I like better than yours."

V. *On closing the mind*. Thou shalt not close thy mind to opposing thoughts, thy ears to opposite truths, thy eyes to other views. "After you used that sexist language, I didn't hear another thing you said."

VI. *On wishful hearing*. Thou shalt not permit thy heart to rule thy mind, nor thy mind thy heart. "I just knew you were going to say that; I had it figured all along."

VII. *On multiple meanings*. Thou shalt not interpret words except as they are interpreted by the speaker. "If I were to stop breathing, would I or would I not expire?"

VIII. *On rehearsing responses.* Thou shalt not use the other's time to prepare responses of your own. "I can't wait until you need a breath! Have I got a comeback for you."

IX. *On fearing challenge.* Thou shalt not fear correction, improvement or change. "I'm talking faster and snowing you because I don't want to hear what you've got to say."

X. *On evading equality.* Thou shalt not over-demand time or fail to claim your own time to hear and be heard.[10]

Listen to others with your heart and not just your head. When you do this you are able to wait for the person to share not only thoughts and feelings but what he or she really means.

Notes

1. George E. Koehler and Nikki Koehler, *My Family: How Shall I Live with It?* (Chicago: Rand McNally and Co., 1968), p. 57, adapted.
2. Ibid., p. 62.
3. Lillian Glass, Ph.D., *Complete Idiot's Guide to Understanding Men and Women* (Indianapolis, IN: Alpha Books, 2000), p. 33, adapted.
4. Dr. Mark Lee, "Why Marriages Fail—Communication," quoted in Gary Collins, ed., *Make More of Your Marriage* (Waco, TX: Word Books, 1976), p. 75.
5. Rebecca Cutter, *When Opposites Attract* (New York: Dutton Books, 1994), pp. 57, 58, adapted.
6. John Ortberg, *Love Beyond Reason* (Grand Rapids, MI: Zondervan, 2000), p. 45 adapted.
7. Aaron T. Beck, *Love Is Not Enough* (New York: Harper and Row, 1988), pp. 74-81, adapted.
8. Deborah Tannen, Ph.D., *You Just Don't Understand* (New York: William Morrow and Co., 1990), pp. 188-192, adapted.
9. Beverly Inman-Ebel, *Talk is Not Cheap* (Austin, TX: Bard Press, 1999), pp. 62, 63, adapted.
10. David Augsburger, *Caring Enough to Hear and Be Heard* (Ventura, CA: Regal Books, 1982), pp. 55-58.

CHAPTER 7

CONNECTION BETWEEN THE GENERATIONS

We've got quite an age range at this company and sometimes that's where we have some of our conflicts. It seems there's a difference in values and in the way to approach problems.

Imagine that you live in a world where everyone is just about your age, give or take five to ten years on either side. Could that be a reality? Well, there are some areas where it seems to be that way. Some newer building developments seem to attract a certain age group, and some of the retirement communities have a grouping on the older end of the scale.

Would you like all of your relationships to be grouped in this way? Probably not, and yet the wider the age range you interact with the greater the possibility for dissension and clashes.

For years, one of the topics of discussion regarding family issues was the generation gap, or how each generation clashed over differences, including their system of values. Today there is still a clash over values among different generations, and these clashes affect every area of our lives.

Years ago, Morris Massey wrote a fascinating book titled *The People Puzzle*.[1] His theory was that we will reflect the values of the decade in which we were 10 years old. What decade was that for you? Was it the '20s, '30s, '40s, '50s, '60s, '70s, '80s? (If you were born in the '90s, you won't be reading this book.) What were the values of your decade? If you were 10 in the '60s, could it be that you sometimes experience conflicts at work because you're dealing with people whose values come from the '40s or from the '80s?

Perhaps differences arise because of varying views on the permanency of marriage or the way money is used or the kind of music each would prefer hearing at work or at church. For instance, does your church have a traditional service and a contemporary service? If so, why both? Couldn't everyone meet together and be satisfied? Probably not. We're used to a certain type of worship and a certain type of music, and we want to remain in this comfort zone.

Problems arise both at church and at work because we are threatened by the differences. We fear what we don't understand; the more we fear something, the less we try to understand it.

When you have a multigenerational situation at work or at church (which we all do) you have the potential for relational disaster. Bring any two generations together and you'll have areas of conflicting values. If that isn't enough, try blending three or four generations together. You can imagine what happens when you have representatives from four generations on your building committee working on the plans for the new sanctuary. (One generation believes that you should only build what you have the cash for, while another generation believes that you should borrow it all and build now).

On a more personal level, how do you handle a family gathering where grandparents in their 80s come face-to-face with the dress, body tattoos, tongue and nose rings of their great-grandkids?

At work, what happens when a cross-generational committee meets to revise policy that includes dress, absenteeism, work hours and office rules, etc? You guessed it. You come up against varying opinions on what is the right thing to do.

LABELING THE GENERATIONS

Let's consider the different generations. Dr. Rick and Kathy Hicks have written a book similar to *The People Puzzle*, but with a Christian perspective. If those in each generation would read *Boomers, Xers and Other Strangers*,[2] getting along would be so much easier. The Hickses' book has provided much of the information in this chapter.

Builders

Numerous names have been suggested to describe the various generations. Several names were suggested for those born before 1946. Who do you know who fits into this grouping? Probably your parents do, or perhaps you do. Because of the traditional values of this group, they have been called *traditionalists*. Many traditionalists fought in World War I and World War II and have been called the *G.I. Generation*. And since they went through the great wars, as they were called, and the Depression, they have also been called the *Survivor Generation*.

In *Boomers, Xers and Other Strangers*, this generational grouping is referred to as *Builders*. These people came back from World War I and began to build a new society. They did the same after the Depression. After World War II they came home to build the economy, cities, highways, railroads and airline companies. The builders were architects and, in other ways, they built our traditional, family-oriented value system.

Boomers

Another group came into being between 1946 and 1964. You've heard the term *Baby Boomers*. Why this label? The population exploded after World War II, and for 18 years this explosion continued. Because of their numbers (76 million), they ended up with a great amount of power and influence.

Gen-Xers

The next generation wasn't so easy to label. Those born between 1965 and 1976 have been called everything from *Generation 13* and *Echo Boomers* to *Baby Busters*. But what we ended up with as a title, more than any of the others, was *Generation X*. Not all of them appreciate this title, either.

N-Gen

The final generation is very young. These are the *Millennials* or *Bridges,* sometimes called *Generation Next*. They were born between 1977 and 1997. You'll find numerous other names used to describe them, including *Net Generation* or *N-Gen*, from the book by Don Tapscott titled *Growing Up Digital—The Rise of the Net Generation*. Members of the *N-Gens* are the first to grow up with access to the Internet.[3]

GENERATIONAL ATTITUDES

Each generation is faced with issues that are different from the previous generation. Children, teens, parents, grandparents—whom do you know from each of these four groups? How are they similar? How do they differ? Which group are you most comfortable with? Which group do you get along with the best?

What are the cross-generational changes that concern you the most or make it more difficult for you to get along with someone?

Differences in values and beliefs can vary to a great degree. Let's take, for example, the Boomers (born between 1946 and 1964) and the Gen-Xers (born between 1965 and 1976) and see why there are differences between these two generational groups.

In some ways the Gen-Xers are a bit like the middle child in a family with a hardworking and recognized firstborn and an attention-getting last-born. The Gen-Xers are squashed between two generational dynasties. Behind them, with their values in place, are over 76 million Boomers. In front of them is the emerging Net Generation, over 80 million strong. The Gen-Xers make up a group of about 46 million.

The Hickses wrote:

They [the Gen-Xers] are the new kids on the block and need to prove themselves, but they're not getting the chance to do so. To older generations, their values seem to be negative, not just different. They don't do things the way Boomers or Builders did, and, therefore, they must be wrong. It's this type of thinking that leads to serious generational tension.[4]

THE WORLD VIEWS OF BOOMERS AND GEN-XERS

The Boomers and Gen-Xers were raised in different environments. Perhaps these differences will shed light on why there is often a lack of harmony in the way they view some issues. Following are some of the main differences delineated by Christian researcher George Barna:

BOOMERS grew up in an era when traditional family values were still cherished by adults.

GEN-Xers grew up in the shadow of their rebellious parents, being more likely to experience an unconventional lifestyle.

BOOMERS were idealistic, believing that people were basically good and that the world was worth saving and improving.

GEN-Xers are not confident in people and institutions They are not sure it's possible to save the world but are trying to do so in order to survive. For example, they grew up with recycling and consider it normal behavior.

BOOMERS believed that the future was waiting to be created. They were optimistic and willing to experiment without fear of failure.

GEN-Xers are world-class skeptics, cynical about mankind and pessimistic about the future.

BOOMERS felt they were a very special people and were entitled to the best the world had to offer.

GEN-Xers feel as if they have been forgotten, if not intentionally limited. They would like to have the best, but realistically have lower expectations.

BOOMERS grew up accepting the possibility of change yet balanced it with a desire for stability.

GEN-Xers have grown up knowing only change. They desire to have influence over the change around them.

BOOMERS matured in a period when information was highly valued but a difficult commodity to obtain.

GEN-Xers have grown up during the information explosion.

BOOMERS were rebellious, but they remained convinced of the value of education.

GEN-Xers view education as something that has to be endured.

BOOMERS have seen work as an end in itself. A significant portion of their identity comes from their status and performance on the job.

GEN-Xers view work as a means to an end. They are not as willing to work long hours to climb the corporate ladder.

BOOMERS have experienced unparalleled economic expansion.

GEN-Xers expect to experience economic parity or decline in comparison with their parents.

BOOMERS defined economic success as achieving greater wealth and prosperity than any other prior generation had ever experienced.

GEN-Xers define economic success as achieving levels of wealth commensurate with that reached by their parents.

BOOMERS have remained an abundantly self-indulgent, bold, and aggressive lot.

GEN-Xers have always felt inferior. Although also selfish and unyielding on principles, their principles are different.

BOOMERS valued relationships but built them in new ways. They were the original networkers, a concept that fit well with their utilitarian view of life and people.

GEN-Xers have outright rejected the impersonal, short-term, fluid relational character of their parents.[5]

Can you imagine being a Builder (perhaps you are a Builder) who manages an office in which most of your employees are Gen-Xers? Or what about being called on to pastor a church or teach a class made up primarily of Gen-Xers? Often I teach graduate classes in which the group will be two-thirds Gen-Xers and one-third Boomers. That's a challenge, since I come in with Builder values and orientation. But I look at this setting in this way: They have something to impart to me and I have something to impart to them. There's a difference between being threatened by these differences and being challenged by them.

There's a difference between feeling threatened by generational differences and being challenged by them.

THE SANDWICHED GENERATION

How would you like to work with a group who feels disillusioned, abandoned and has a defensive manner? George Barna's survey findings show that these are the views of Gen-Xers.

Why are they skeptical? Because they've experienced deception and superficiality. (How much of this have you experienced in life and what was its impact upon you?) Why do they feel abandoned? Because they are living in a depleted world and believe they are being cheated out of the wealth that would have been theirs with more careful stewardship from the previous generation, and they resent being emotionally neglected by their parents. This also contributes to their defensiveness—they expected more than they're going to get. It's a competitive world, so don't trust others.

If you're of a different generation than the Xer, how do you respond to these attitudes and beliefs when you encounter them?

WORKPLACE TENSION

The various generations are actually living through profound changes in the workplace. The older a person is, the more disruptive it can be, especially with technological globalization and downsizing. Add to this a 23-year-old, 42-year-old, 56-year-old and a 64-year old working in the same office. Without flexibility you have constant collisions.

Gen-Xers aren't keen on gradually working their way to the top. Bruce Tulgan, author of *Managing Generation X: How to Bring Out the Best in Young Talent* (W. W. Norton), talks about them not wanting to do things the old way but definitely wanting to do plenty in a new way.

Ron Zemke, coauthor of *Generations at Work* (Amacom), points out that the greatest conflicts occur between Baby Boomers and Gen-Xers. Boomers see work as an end in itself, whereas Gen-Xers see it as a means to an end. They would rather have a killer lifestyle than a killer job. In general, Gen-Xers have a short attention span and like constant stimulation as well as new challenges. And their preference is for verbal instructions over reading; and above all, keep it short and simple.[6]

How An Xer Approaches Life

Gen-Xers do not want to wait; they want a high quality of life now. That also means life is fun without sacrifice. I've seen this attitude in some couples in my premarital counseling. They want to bring their marriage to the same economic level it has taken their parents 30 years of work to attain. They don't realize they'll be stepping down in their lifestyle when they marry and will need to do so if they want to avoid further debt. I talk with many who are finally facing the reality of their $75,000 school loans at 8 percent interest. When you're taking money in college, you don't think about payback time.

Barna's studies indicate that Gen-Xers are independent and make their own decisions, are comfortable with change and aren't concerned about traditions. When they do commit, the commitments are more meaningful than those the Boomer makes. Different viewpoints do not threaten them. In fact, diversity in many areas is very comfortable. They're a flexible group; and when it comes to absolutes, there are few.

If you're a traditionalist (the old term), or Builder, do you think you would be comfortable discussing politics, male-female relationships, theology or the teaching of Paul in one of his epistles with Gen-Xers?

Gen-Xers play by different rules than other generations. In his book *Generation Next*, Barna lists 15 new rules by which this generation will play:

New Rule #1: Personal relationships count. Institutions don't.

New Rule #2: The process is more important than the product.

New Rule #3: Aggressively pursue diversity among people.

New Rule #4: Enjoying people and life opportunities is more important than productivity, profitability, or achievement.

New Rule #5: Change is good.

New Rule #6: The development of character is more crucial than achievement.

New Rule #7: You can't always count on your family to be there for you, but it is your best hope for emotional support.

New Rule #8: Each individual must assume responsibility for his or her own world.

New Rule #9: Whenever necessary, gain control—and use it wisely.

New Rule #10: Don't waste time searching for absolutes. There are none.

New Rule #11: One person can make a difference in the world—but not much.

New Rule #12: Life is hard and then we die; but because it's the only life we've got, we may as well endure it, enhance it, and enjoy it as best we can.

New Rule #13: Spiritual truth may take many forms.

New Rule #14: Express your rage.

New Rule #15: Technology is our natural ally.[7]

GENERATIONAL VIEWS
OF FAMILY

Let's consider some of the other differences between the generational groups. What about the role of mothers? How could this ever be a problem? A mother is a mother, isn't she? Most Builders believed that a mother's place is in the home with the children. Boomers, Gen-Xers and N-Gens feel that mothers should have the option to stay at home or work wherever and whenever they want to.

Views concerning the extended family vary as well. Builders believe it's best to all live near each other. When their Boomer children scatter, they feel a bit frustrated. There are also differences on how the next generation is raising and indulging their children. Builders tended to pour themselves into their children; Gen-Xers were the first to more or less raise themselves. "Latchkey kids" became the phrase of this time period. No wonder they felt abandoned by adults. But so many had only one parent whose work was a necessity. The Net Generation tends to see the single parent or blended household (second marriages that result in stepparents, stepchildren and stepsiblings) as the norm. In fact, by 2007 there will be more blended-family households than nuclear households in our country.

Consider the different values when it comes to marriage. For Builders, marriage means "until death us do part." For Boomers, divorce is a solution when there are too many problems in a relationship. This model for the Gen-Xers has resulted in their fear of marriage. They delay marriage and engage in the great American experiment—living together. This option has been a major flop in helping marriages stay together. Every research study conducted has delivered the same results on people who live together and then marry—a much higher divorce rate than the national average and a higher conflict level, as well as abuse.

Money Matters

Can you see how some of these value differences make getting along a bit more of a challenge? Many differences not only divide families, but they also create tension in the workplace and at church. How and when funds are used or handled can be a reflection of generational val-ues. Builders want to save it because "you never know when there's going to be another depression." That's the message they grew up with. Boomers were raised with money, so if it's there, spend it, and spend it now. If you need more money, go back and borrow it (or attempt to) from your saver parents. This is a major genera-tional conflict.

You would think that each generation would continue to have more and more money. But with the Gen-Xers it isn't so. They have the same wants as

Those in the field of marketing have paid close attention to the various generations and their values to better direct their presentations to each group.

the Boomers, but the Boomers have the good jobs and aren't about to give them up. There's tension between these two groups since the Gen-Xers feel excluded. The N-Gens have a new means to serve their need for instant gratification—the Internet.

Those in the field of marketing have paid close attention to the various generations and their values. By knowing their pur-chasing patterns, marketers can better direct their presentations to each group.

The only group that wasn't catered to, at first, was the Builders. But this group's needs have now evolved into a share of the marketplace. Boomers, however, have always been targeted by industries. The motto has long been "Find out what they want and give it to them." You can see how this concept was applied in the church as the seeker-friendly approach has gained a foothold. Some Builders sit by and shake their heads. Others realize that some changes need to be made in the format and content of church services, but they attend a traditional service themselves.

Gen-Xers once again are left out a bit since they aren't as strong in number as the Boomers. Not as many gadgets are geared to them. They've even been called the "ignored market."[8]

BRIDGING THE DIFFERENCES

How do we bridge the generational differences? The first step is to acknowledge and understand them. Understanding means comprehending the meaning of the differences, but it also means having a tolerant attitude toward them. You are partly the way you are today because of the time and environment in which you were raised. Your life experiences have impacted you. It's the same with other generations. My Boomer daughter has been my teacher and helped me to better understand her generation as well as the Gen-Xers.

Morris Massey, in *The People Puzzle*, shows us how understanding can work in the context of generational and values differences:

> The gut-level value systems are, in fact, dramatically different between the generations that presently exist simultaneously in our society. The focus should not be so much on how to change other people to conform to our standards, our values. Rather, we must learn how to accept and understand other people in their own right, acknowledging the validity of their values, their behavior.

American Indians believed that to know another man you must walk a mile in his moccasins. This is a classic challenge for understanding others. If we can understand and respect other people and their values, then we can interact with them in a more effective manner.[9]

It's so easy to prejudge others who are different from us. When we do this, communication and getting along is hindered. When you make a snap judgment about a differing group, your vision begins to change. You develop a narrow focus that only looks for evidence to support your beliefs and discards anything to the contrary. An open ear, an open mind and an open heart will help us all to understand things we have never understood before. We may not agree with another generation's lifestyle or values, but understanding them helps us to package and present what we would like to share with them.[10]

Notes

1. Morris E. Massey, *The People Puzzle* (New York: Prentice Hall, 1980).
2. Dr. Rick and Kathy Hicks, *Boomers, Xers and Other Strangers* (Colorado Springs, CO and Wheaton, IL: Focus on the Family and Tyndale House, 1999), pp. 304, 305, adapted.
3. Ibid., pp. 229-231, adapted.
4. Ibid., pp. 254.
5. George Barna, *Baby Busters: The Disillusioned Generation* (Chicago: Northfield Publishing, 1994), pp. 72-74.
6. Shawn Taylor, "Negotiating Differences in Age," *Los Angeles Times,* January 14, 2000, p. W1.
7. Barna, *Generation Next* (Ventura, CA: Regal Books, 1995), p. 46.
8. Hicks, *Boomers, Xers and Other Strangers,* pp. 292, 293, adapted.
9. Morris Massey, *The People Puzzle,* p. 21.
10. Hicks, *Boomers, Xers and Other Strangers,* pp. 322, 323, adapted.

CHAPTER 8

THE DIFFERENT WAYS PEOPLE LEARN

I wonder about some of the people in my office. When I explain things to them
they understand immediately. But the information doesn't seem to connect
with others until I give them the same input in writing. It's hard to
figure out why people are so different.

I know the answer to this question before I ask it, but I'll ask you
anyway. Would you like people at church and at work to listen to
you, consider what you have to say and be influenced by your
words? Of course you would. Who wouldn't? It will happen if
you develop the skill to be flexible enough to communicate in
such a way that you really connect with others. This is best done
by learning to speak another person's language.

People like to talk to those who speak in the same language
style. If this is at the heart of the communication process in marriage and with family, it will also work with coworkers, employ-

ees, employers, board and committee members, small group participants and friends.

Have you ever thought of what speaking another person's language entails? There are several facets to this process. You need to discover how the people around you learn and then choose a way of speaking that matches that learning style. We do this all the time as parents or teachers of children. And it works.

Our learning styles do not really change much from the time we were children. We still need the same things as adults. It doesn't take that much effort to understand a person's learning style and give him what he needs.

If you would like to be heard, if you would like to be a catalyst in the lives of others, if you would like others to really enjoy your presence and if you would like to get along with others, here is what you can do.

IDENTIFYING A PERSON'S LEARNING STYLE

To learn how to speak other people's languages, begin to observe your coworkers or those you work with at church. Observe their patterns of behavior. When are they successful? When do they make progress, and what happened to make that progress occur?

Next, listen to the way they communicate. How do they phrase what they say? What type of words do they use? What do you hear in terms of their thinking style? How do you speak to the other person? Are you connecting or do you both sound like you're speaking a foreign language? If you listen well, you can connect with another person by learning how to repackage what you say. This concept is expressed well by Pastor Dr. Holland London. He said, "People often ask me why I take so many detours when I speak. I just tell them it's because I'm trying to reach those who don't live on the highway." Too many times we end up trying to get others around us to move onto our highway so that we don't have to put up with the inconvenience of detours.[1]

After you have identified a person's language style, experiment to discover his or her learning style. It could be totally different from yours, and that's all right. As you experiment and learn about others, you will find yourself (hopefully) trying some approaches you have never tried before. Not only will you surprise others when you do this, but you will also end up surprising yourself.

The way we learn is a reflection of how we solve problems. If you would like to assist others in problem solving, discover their learning styles.

The way we learn is a reflection of how we solve problems. If you would like to assist others in problem solving, discover their learning styles.

ELEMENTS THAT AFFECT LEARNING

Let's consider some other factors that most people never think about when it comes to learning. Where, when and how a person learns describe his or her environmental preferences.

Time of day is one environmental preference. Research studies have been consistent in their results. There is a particular time of day or night when you are not at your best. There is also a time when you are the most productive. When do you tackle your most difficult tasks during the day? Is this the best timing for you? Perhaps you hit your prime time of learning at 11 P.M.; or it could be that you're an early morning individual and that's your prime time for learning and production.

What about your coworkers? Do some hit the office running at 8 A.M., with high productivity that drops in the afternoon? Are there some who do not hit their stride until early afternoon? When is your best time of day? It's important for you do determine this, since we tend to think others' high productivity time should match our own. When it doesn't, difficulties in getting along may arise.

I'm an early morning person. To me it's the best time of the day. And since I'm alert and functional at this time, I used to assume that everyone else who is ambulatory was alert then as well. That's not quite true.

A number of years ago, I had an office manager who would arrive at 8:30. She was energetic and an excellent worker. A few minutes after she arrived, I would come in with a list for the day. I had already been working and was into my stride. Since she was there, I just assumed that she would be at the same level. She wasn't. I soon made an adjustment. When she arrived I would just greet her and then back off and give her space for the first hour. During this time she could become alert in her own timing. Often about an hour later she would come into my office with a list and say, "OK, Norm, let's look at what needs to be done today. I've got a list . . ." We learned to work together well.

Intake is another factor that affects learning. Some do not do their best work unless they have something to eat or drink while they're concentrating. To others this appears messy or distracting. What about you? What helps you to learn?

Lighting is another factor. Some people need a very bright environment in which to work, while others need softer illumination. What preferences do you see in your work environment?

If people have to work in a setting that affects their eyes in a negative way, they don't do their best work.

Temperature is yet another factor. Most of us have a certain temperature range at which we work best. The problem occurs when different needs arise. I've seen classes and board meetings at church in which different individuals would either raise or lower the window or fiddle with the temperature controls every few minutes because they weren't comfortable.

Because I conduct seminars in various settings across the country, I am very conscious of both lighting and temperature, especially the latter. I've noticed that women react to the cold much more readily than men and are usually the ones who want the temperature raised. For a learning environment, it's best if it's a bit more brisk than too warm (especially after lunch). There's less tendency to doze off when you're cool.[2]

HOW WE SENSE THE WORLD

What we're going to consider now is perhaps the most important part of this chapter: how we take in information. All of the previous information we've covered needs to be considered and incorporated into our thinking with this aspect of learning and remembering. Let's illustrate with a conversation between three men at work.

One says to his two friends, "Everyone knows that seeing is believing."

The man next to him replies, "Oh, no, Fred, hearing is believing."

"I hate to inform you," the third man counters, "but you're both wrong. Feeling is believing."

Who is right? They all are. For some people, seeing is believing; for others hearing is believing; and for a third group, feeling or sensing is believing.

How do you respond to life? Do you *see* things more? Do you *hear* things more? Do you sense or *feel* things more? We all respond to what is occurring around us in one of these three ways. Our perception of the world is created through our visual, auditory, kinesthetic (sensory) and olfactory/gustatory (smell and taste) senses. Because of certain influences upon us and our experiences with our environment, we tend to develop or lean upon one of these senses or intake systems more than the others. We use them all, but we rely more heavily upon one. This preference is the engine that drives the way we learn.

Sensory Distinctions
If you are an auditory person, you tend to rely on spoken words for your information. If you are visually oriented, you use your eyes to perceive the world around you and use visual images in remembering and thinking. If you're a kinesthetically oriented individual, you tend to feel your way through your experiences. Both internal and external stimuli are sorted through your sensory feelings and these feelings determine your decisions. In our culture, very few people rely solely on the senses of smell and taste.

An individual in a scientific profession would have an easier time if his or her dominant mode of perception was visual rather than kinesthetic. Having sensory feelings about scientific formulas or equations is not really going to prove very helpful. On the other hand, someone who studies ballet will find it easier to master if he or she has a highly developed kinesthetic sense.

When I was in junior high school, the band and orchestra members took tests each year. We listened to various tones and pitches to determine our ability. Some students made some very fine auditory distinctions; these individuals had an auditory bent or inclination. The intake system we use will affect the way we respond to and cope with life.

Even though we prefer to experience life through one dominant sense, we may increase the use of our other senses as well. For a number of reasons, I have learned to do this over the years. My primary sensing apparatus has been visual. I'm not sure why, except that I know it was highly emphasized and reinforced when I was a child. I read extensively and undoubtedly that helped to create the imaginative pictures in my mind. I also learned to sight-read music very well between the ages of 6 and 16. At times I am still frustrated by individuals who cannot read a note of music. Yet if you hum a tune for them, they may be able to play 15 variations on that theme. My orientation is visual. Theirs is auditory.

My visual side frequently comes to the forefront. If one of my secretaries comes into my office and says, "Norm, here's an interesting letter. Let me read it to you." Without thinking I will respond, "Oh, let me see it." I like to read things for myself because I process them faster that way. Invariably I ask people to send it to me in writing or to put suggestions in writing and turn them in to me so I can see them.

Recently I heard the story of several office employees who felt frustrated about their inability to get their requests and ideas across to a vice president. They approached the man and talked with him, and at times he appeared interested, but nothing ever came of their time spent with him. When three of these employees discussed the problem with their office manager, he made a simple suggestion: "It isn't as though your ideas aren't good. They just aren't registering with him. I think he's a person who, like it or not, needs everything to come to his attention in writing. I know this means a little extra work for you, but let's try to present everything in writing. This doesn't mean that you can't share your ideas in person; but at the same time have it typed out in detail, and then let's see what happens."

The employees grumbled a bit but followed the suggestion. Were they ever surprised when their ideas, which their boss had apparently discarded before, were now accepted! Why? Because the vice president was a visual person and liked to have his information in writing. When his employees began to talk his language, he began to listen.

When I hear new ideas or concepts, whether they are simple or complex, my visual side kicks in and I think, *How can I diagram these concepts and put them on an overhead transparency so I can convey them better to those I teach?*

THE VOCABULARY OF EACH SENSORY PREFERENCE

Let's summarize what I've been *saying* to *see* if you're in *touch* with it yet. (Notice I used words for all three senses.) We have three main senses—hearing, seeing and feeling. We prefer to use one sense over the other two for perceiving life, storing our experiences and making decisions. How do we discover which sense we prefer? Our *language* gives it away.

The visual person uses terms like:

I *see* what you're saying.
That *looks* good to me.
I'm not too *clear* on this right now.
This is still a bit *hazy* to me.
Boy, when they asked that question, I just went *blank*.
That sheds a new *light* on the problem.
Do you pick up my *perspective*?

Here are some of the most typical words you will hear coming from the visual person:

focus	colorful
see	pretty
clear	peek
bright	glimpse
picture	imagine
perspective	notice
show	hazy

The auditory person uses terms like:

That *rings* a bell with me.
It *sounds* real good to me.
I *hear* you.
I'm trying to *tune* in what you're saying.
Listen to this new idea.
I had to *ask* myself.
That idea *clicks* with me.

Here are some of the typical words you will hear coming from an auditory person:

listen	loud
call	shout
talk	told
hear	tone
harmony	sounds
noisy	say
discuss	amplify

The kinesthetic person will use phrases such as these:

I can't get a *handle* on this.
I've got a good *feeling* about this project.
Can you get in *touch* with what I'm saying?
It's easy to *flow* with what they're saying.
I don't *grasp* what you're trying to do.
This is a *heavy* situation.

Some of the typical words used are:

feel	irritated
firm	clumsy

touch	pushy
pressure	relaxed
tense	grab
concrete	soft
hurt	handle
touch	smooth
know	need
think	experience
remember	decide
change	negotiate
want	pretend

Which of the three senses do you prefer to use? Had you ever considered this idea of sensory preference? I find it easy to close my eyes and picture in my mind an experience from the past or an anticipated experience. When I read a novel, I see the action in my mind in vivid color and could describe all the visual details. But this would be difficult for some people. Vice versa, I might find it difficult to experience the smell of a flower in my mind. I could work at it, but for others it would be easy. Some people can hear the sound of life all around them just by thinking about it. Some individuals have very vivid mental images, others have faded images and some have none at all. Some of us see sentences in our minds.

As you talk with people, you may wonder which sense is their dominant one. How can you discover this? There are times when it really isn't apparent and you won't know at first which form of communication will work best. So you need to experiment. If you aren't sure which sensing mode is dominant for a person, vary your questions. Ask "Does this idea *look* all right to you?" "How do you *feel* about investing in this new program?" If one approach doesn't seem to work, switch to another.

What we sometimes perceive as resistance on the part of other people may not be resistance at all. *We're just not speaking their language.* Sometimes it helps to ask people how they would like the information presented. They will appreciate your sensitivity and your willingness to learn their language.

One man approached me and said, "Norm, I would like to go over this new program with you, and I can do it in two ways. I can let you see it first and read over the summary pages and then you can ask me questions, or I can sit down with you and explain it step-by-step. Which would you prefer?" Which one do you think I chose? You're right. I read the pages and then asked questions.

A sales representative approached me one day and said, "Norm, I have this new testing program you've just got to hear about. I've been looking forward to telling you all about it so you can really get a feel for what we're going to be doing." I wasn't as positive about this person's approach. But someone else from the same company called later and said, "Norm, I've been wondering if you would be interested in learning about our new program. You might want to see where we're going. I can do two things. I can give you a brief summary over the phone, and then you can let me know how it looks to you and we can proceed in more detail. Or I can stop by with an overview and go through the entire program step-by-step. Which would you prefer?" He spoke my language by using terminology and giving me a choice.

Let's look now at some conversations between people with different learning styles, either *visual*, *kinesthetic* or *auditory*.

Visual: "Jim, if you would look over that new room arrangement again, you will see that I've taken your needs into consideration. I have focused on the important places in the room. It looks good to me. I don't see what you're so bothered about."

Kinesthetic: "I don't know . . . I just keep getting the feeling that something about it is wrong. I've just got this sense about it. You know, I can't put my finger on it, it's just a bit uncomfortable."

Visual: "Oh, come on. Look at it from my perspective. The room is brighter this way and we have more walking space. Stand over here and look around the room."

Kinesthetic: "I don't know. I don't think you're in touch with how I feel about this room. I just can't get a handle on it, but if we leave it this way, it just isn't going to work."

What is happening in this conversation? We have two points of view. But the main problem is that they're talking right past each other. They aren't connecting. One uses words referring to how she see things, and the other uses words to reflect how he feels. Let's listen in on another discussion between a visual and an auditory learner.

Auditory: "John, I want to talk with you about something that we've spoken about before. I know we're ready to move on the room addition, but I've still got some ideas, and I want to know how these sound to you. Now, please hear me out, because they are a bit involved."

Visual: "Do you have them outlined for me? Let me see them first, and then we can act on them. That will save a lot of time, since I've got a lot going on right now."

Auditory: "Well, they're not finalized yet. I've just started to tune into them and I thought we could discuss them. You know, I do want to have some say in the final outcome."

Visual: "Oh, I agree. You need to have your views reflected in this new addition. But for me to focus in on what you're trying to present, I would like you to give me something definite to see. Why don't you formulate it clearly and then let's talk."

Again there is miscommunication. They're talking two different languages, but if one or both could change, they would connect.

DISCOVERING A PERSON'S LEARNING MODE

If you're wondering what someone's learning mode is—whether visual, auditory or kinesthetic—you could try a variety of responses in conversation with the person to help you discover his or her way of responding to life.

Visual statements or questions include:

- It appears to you . . .
- You see it in this way . . .
- Do you see it that way?
- How does it appear to you?

Kinesthetic statements or questions include:

- You are sort of feeling that . . .
- You are communicating a sense of . . .
- I somehow sense that you feel . . .
- Are you saying this makes you feel . . . ?

Auditory statements and questions include:

- Listening to you, it seems as if . . .
- I really hear you saying . . .
- What would you like to express to her . . . ?
- I kind of hear you saying that . . .

Over the years I've tried to include phrases from all three styles when I teach so that I can reach everyone. Remember that a visual person is more comfortable talking with another visual, an auditory with another auditory and a kinesthetic with another kinesthetic.

PACING A CONVERSATION

Now let's look at an example of a conversation that includes you and see if you can tell what makes the difference.

Visual: "As I look over these plans for the new room arrangement you showed me, I have some questions about it. I'm just not clear where we are going to put all of the old and new furniture."

You: "Well, I think I can see where your concern is coming from. Maybe it's not all that clear to me either, but let me try to paint a picture of what's inside my head. I guess I need to illustrate this for both of us so we can discover the solution."

Auditory: "John, let's talk some more about the new addition. I listened to your thoughts last night, and since I've had some time to consider them, I wonder if we're really on the same wavelength. Now, here's what I want to say."

You: "All right, I hear you. I'll try to tune into your thoughts about this room. I want it to be comfortable for both of us. I sure want us to be in harmony over this room, since we have to live with it for the next few years."

Kinesthetic: "I'm sorry, but I just can't seem to get in touch with what you're saying. It just isn't concrete enough for me to grab. I want this room to feel comfortable to me and everyone else. So far what you've been describing just doesn't seem to fit."

You: "Well, I understand what you're feeling. We are connecting on this, even though it doesn't feel that way for you."

What happened in these conversations? They were more successful because your character *paced* the conversation—you were able to fit your vocabulary to the other person's. This is a classic example of speaking the other person's language. In fact, this was an example of *translation*. You translated your language to fit that of the other person. Pacing, or translating, is a skill you can learn to use when talking with other people.

Let's consider this approach in the field of business. Here is an example concerning the presentation of a house to prospective buyers. As you read the three descriptions below, which house would appeal to you the most?

1. This house is quite picturesque, with a quaint look about it. You can see that a lot of focus has been put on the colorful patio and garden area. The house has a lot of window space to allow you to enjoy the view. It is clearly a good buy.
2. This house is soundly constructed and well situated. It is in such a quiet area that all you hear when you walk outside are the sounds of the birds singing. Its storybook interior has so much character you'll probably be asking yourself how you could ever pass it by.
3. This house is not only solidly constructed, it has a special feel to it. It's not often you come in contact with a place that touches on so many features. It is spacious enough that you feel you can move around

freely, yet cozy enough that you won't wear yourself
out taking care of it.[3]

Pacing includes the verbal aspects of communication, using
the same or similar terminology as the person to whom you are
talking. You simply meet the person where he or she is and
match his language in some way. For instance, have you ever
found yourself slowing your rate of speech or picking up the
pace because of the other person's speech pattern? Pacing also
includes the volume level of speech. If you speak softly, you usually appreciate someone else who also speaks softly. If someone
speaks loudly, you soon discover that he respects you more for
speaking at his volume level.

Pacing Builds Rapport
In some way the goal of all communication is to build understanding—rapport—with another person. Pacing verbal communication is the key to building rapport. I heard a story of a man
who used pacing in his contacts over the phone to increase his
sales. He owned an answering service, and since he was familiar
with the concept of pacing, he began to match the rate of speed
of people who called in for information. He needed to make his
phone conversations count, since this was basically his only contact. If the inquirer spoke rather slowly, he spoke slowly; if the
inquirer spoke quickly, so did the salesman. He was pleasantly
surprised to discover a 30-percent increase in his subscription
rate, just from pacing his telephone conversations.

THE EYES HAVE IT
I have found the study of neuro-linguistic psychology (NLP) to
be very helpful in my role as a counselor. NLP, developed by two
professors (Bandler and Grinder) at UC Santa Cruz in the 1970s,

covers a vast area, but much of it, as you will see in this chapter, involves external clues to internal states. Although NLP includes the study of posture and body movement, it encompasses more subtle indicators of a person's thoughts and emotions—for example, the significance of eye movement.

Have you ever talked to someone and noticed the person's eyes stray from looking at you directly? Perhaps the person glanced up and to the right for a moment or looked down and to the right. Have you been in a classroom setting, either as a participant or as a teacher, and noticed one of the class members gazing upward and to the left? Have you ever noticed the eye movements of two individuals as they carry on a conversation?

The eye movements of a child or an adult are not random movements. They have a specific purpose. Perhaps you've wondered if lack of eye contact means that a person might be indicating he is uncomfortable, simply is not listening or is daydreaming. There are other possibilities. Watching people's eyes as you converse with them, or even when you speak in front of a group, gives you a clue as to what they are thinking about. Does that sound like mind reading? Before you dismiss this idea, read on. Listening with our eyes is an undeveloped skill for most of us; but this information will make you a better listener.

Eye movements are a doorway to a person's thoughts. For example, if a person shifts his eyes up and to the right, he is in the process of *constructing a visual image*.

If a person shifts his eyes
up and to the left, he is *recalling some
previous images*.

If an individual keeps
her eyes level and to the right, she is in
the process of *constructing sounds*.

If the person keeps his eyes
level and shifts them to the left, he is
remembering previously heard sounds.

If the individual looks
down and to the right, she is
experiencing feelings.

If the person is looking down
and to the left, he is probably
talking to himself.

(Many left-handed individuals
will be reversed right to left with
respect to these charts).[4]

If the study of eye movements seems like a radical idea, let me give you an example from my counseling experience with a man I'll call Frank. During a discussion with him, I noticed that Frank looked up and to the left when he was *remembering* the *look* on his wife's face when he gave her a gift. As he talked about what he thought would happen as a result of taking his wife on a surprise trip, he looked up and to the right as he *constructed an image* of how she would respond. Later on in our discussion he looked down and to the left as he *talked to himself* about either of the previous pictures. As he *recalled a time* when his wife *shared* with him how much she loved him, he looked straight and level, but to the left. As he *constructed different ways* of sharing with his wife how much she means to him, he looked straight and level and to the right. As he *experienced the feeling* of being loved, he looked down and to the right.

What does all this mean? *The more observant you are, the more sensitive you will become and the better you can communicate and get along with others.*

FINE-TUNING YOUR ABILITY TO CONVERSE

Let's consider this approach in the field of business. Let's say a customer and a real-estate agent have been talking for some time. The customer moves her eyes level and to the left and says, "I just keep getting the feeling that something is missing from this. But I can't put my finger on it." Look back at the suggestions concerning eye movement. Is the customer constructing new pictures, feeling something, talking to herself, or remembering images and pictures? She is probably remembering or hearing something. The agent who is sensitive to this responds by saying, "Well, I'm glad you told me that. Is there something we will need to *talk* about? Are you still concerned about the *noise* problem in this neighborhood?"

In our conversations with people, the proper use of questions can encourage them to share what they are experiencing as well as convey to them our sensitivity to their feelings and circumstances. Too often we use general questions such as, "What are you thinking?" or "What are you feeling?" which may miss the mark. If the person you are talking to shifts his eyes up and to the right, how would you respond? You might say, "I wonder what picture is coming to your mind at this time?" or, "I wonder what it looks like to you?"

If the person looks up and to the left you could say, "I wonder what picture from your photo album is coming to your mind at this time?" If the person looks to the right but her eyes are level, you could say, "Perhaps you're beginning to hear how this sounds."

If the person is looking level and to the left, a question like, "How did that sound to you when you first heard it expressed?" would be appropriate. Or, "Do you remember hearing her make that statement to you?"

When the individual looks down and to the right you might respond with, "It appears you might be feeling something at this time," or "I would like to catch the feeling you're experiencing at this time," or "You appear to be sensing something at this moment."

As the person looks down and to the left you could respond, "If I could listen into your mind right now, what would you be saying?"

Perhaps the information in this chapter is shockingly new to you and you have a difficult time accepting it. Before you make your final decision about its validity, however, give the ideas a try. As you are willing to change your style of communication and become more flexible, your communication with others may be revolutionized!

Notes

1. Cynthia Ulrich Tobias, *The Way They Learn: How to Discover and Teach to Your Child's Strengths* (Wheaton, IL: Tyndale House Publishers, 1996), pp. 7-9, adapted.
2. Ibid., pp. 185-190, adapted.
3. Robert B. Dilts, *Applications of Neuro-Linguistic Programming to Business Communication* (Cupertino, CA: Meta Publications, 1983), n.p.
4. For another book on this subject, see Jerry Richardson, *The Magic of Rapport* (Cupertino, CA: Meta Publications, 1988), pp. 75-98, adapted.

CHAPTER 9

COMMUNICATION CHALLENGES BETWEEN MEN AND WOMEN

*Look at the funny titles of books today about men and women—*Men are From Mars and Women Are From Venus! *What's next?* Men Are From Moab and Women Are From Boaz?. . . Men Are Like Clams, Women Are Like Crowbars?. . . *Give me a break! Is there really such a difference?*

"It was like a college education. For five years I was the only woman executive with the corporation and I worked with seven other male executives. When I entered that level I felt like an outsider. It was a very structured world because of the type of company it was.

"I did learn to adjust to their structure, their way of thinking and especially to their style of talking. But at first my feelings were

shattered. There was a lack of sensitivity. Praise in public and criticism in private was not practiced. Sometimes these men seemed
so blunt and direct that I felt like crumbling inside. But I learned
not to take it personally. It was just the way they talked. And when
I began to communicate in their style, they heard me. It really
turned into a good experience.

"A couple of them learned to modify their approach when
they talked with me. The others just remained the way they
always were. I discovered that the two men who modified their
communication got along better with everyone and were well
liked as well as respected. The principle I learned in five years was
'those who flex have influence and get along.'"

What this woman shared with me has been experienced by
many people.

There are major changes in the gender composition of the
work world outside the home. Women now make up over 45 percent of the work force and 35 percent of managerial positions.
Women business owners now employ more people than all the
Fortune 500 companies put together.[1]

Dr. Judith Tingley, author of *Genderflex*,™ comments on the
major adjustment between men and women in the work place:

> Men and women are literally at war now in the work-
> place. The gender battle is no longer under wraps.
> Sometimes it's a cold war, discussed in hushed tones
> with solutions pursued only in private. At other times,
> the verbal assaults explode into tempers and hurt feel-
> ings. But everyone understands that there is conflict.
> Few people tread lightly. Women are male-bashing pub-
> licly, men are female-bashing privately. Out-and-out sur-
> vival has become a daily scenario. It has become "them
> or us"—without much thought for tomorrow and how
> this conflict will continue to affect American business
> growth and productivity.[2]

Do you remember when you learned to drive a car? Many years ago most of us learned on stickshifts primarily because very few cars had automatic transmissions. The gearshift was on the steering column or on the floor. It was tricky, learning to coordinate the pushing of the clutch as you shifted from one gear to the next. If you did it right, it went smoothly and quietly. If not, you ground the gears. You could hear as well as feel the metal clashing and grinding. If you did this often enough you would grind the gears into fine pieces of metal, eventually ruining the transmission.

A similar thing can happen to two people who continually collide. You can end up grinding and clashing against one another.

THE NEED FOR UNDERSTANDING AND ADAPTATION

Aside from the meshing that needs to occur, another major issue comes into play when you seek to learn each other's culture: the blending of your gender (maleness/femaleness) and personality differences. This is a major step in learning to speak each other's language.

Too often gender differences are reduced to one factor, such as personality preferences or being left- or right-brained. It actually makes more sense to look at men and women as a complex mixture of differences. In that way you can understand them better.

Understanding and adapting to a coworker's personality—which includes gender uniqueness as well as brain dominance and personality—will make the difference as to whether or not each person adjusts to the foreigner! When two people are in sync, the gears do not grind when they shift in a relationship, and the communication between the two is a positive experience with increased productivity.

To make this happen, each person needs to accept two facts:

1. Men and women are wired differently. Neither is wired wrong, just differently.
2. In order to work in harmony, men and women need to become "bilingual," each fluent in the language of the opposite sex.

Several years ago, my wife and I had an experience that dramatically portrayed gender differences in both thinking and communication style. We were visiting historical Williamsburg in Virginia, a fascinating and charming setting that preserves our colonial history.

One day we decided to take the tour of the old governor's mansion. The tour guide was a man. As we entered the large entry door, he began to give a factual description of the purpose of the room as well as the way it was furnished. He described in detail the various ancient guns on the wall and pointed to the unique display of flintlock rifles arranged in a circle on the rounded ceiling. When he said there were 64 of them, some originals and others replicas, I immediately began counting them (which is a typical male response—we're into numbers). The guide was very knowledgeable and he gave an excellent detailed description as we went from room to room. He seemed to be very structured and focused.

We had to leave before the tour was completed to meet some friends for lunch. Since we both enjoyed the presentation so much, we decided to return the next day and take the tour again. What a difference! This day the guide was a woman. We entered the same room and she said, "Now you'll notice a few guns on the wall and ceiling, but notice the covering on these chairs and the tapestry on the walls, they are . . ." And with that she launched into a detailed description of items that had either been ignored or just given a passing mention the day before. And on it went throughout the tour.

It didn't take much to figure out what was going on. It was a classic example of gender differences. The first tour guide was speaking more to men than to women, and the second one spoke more to women than to men. Actually, we ended up with the best tour imaginable because we heard both perspectives. What a benefit it would be if the guides would incorporate both perspectives into their presentations!

As we consider some of the unique characteristics of men and women, we need to keep two things in mind. First, there are *some generalizations that pertain to most men and women*. But there will *always be exceptions, in varying degrees*. Second, *the way men and women are wired is not negative*. It is not a fault to be one way or the other. Some gender characteristics will be more pronounced in some people because of personality type as well as upbringing. The problem arises when people feel they are always right or the way they do things is the only right way. They don't seem to care about understanding and accepting the opposite sex for the way they are. The more flexibility people develop, the better they will be able to work together.[3]

It's not easy to flex and learn to respond differently; but it's possible. What is second nature for you has to be a conscious effort on the other's part, and vice versa.

Many men and women say they know about the differences between the genders, such as feeling vs. fact, brain differences, energy levels, etc. But their interaction often leads to this question: If they know the differences, why do they keep fighting something that is a natural and inherited ability, as well as having been designed by God Himself?

If people really knew the differences between male and female styles of thinking and communicating, then they would be able to explain the differences in detail and accept them. They would honor the differences and respond in an appropriate and accepting way.

BRAIN FUNCTIONING DIFFERENCES IN MEN AND WOMEN

The following may seem like a basic course in biology, physiology and anthropology, but it's simply an explanation of some basic gender differences that most people still allow to confuse them and dictate their responses to the opposite sex.

Much of the mystery is solved when you understand the less obvious physiological differences between men and women. When Scripture says that God created them male and female, He really did create us differently: "Now the Lord said, 'It is not good (sufficient, satisfactory) that the man should be alone; I will make him a helper meet (suitable, adapted, complementary) for him" (Genesis 2:18, *AMP*). And many of the unapparent differences are found in the brain.

Let's take a look at the brain.

The left hemisphere controls language and reading skills. It gathers up information and processes it logically in a step-by-step fashion. When is the left brain used? Every day when you read a book or article, play a game, sing, write, balance your checkbook and weigh the advantages and disadvantages of buying an item on time versus paying cash.

If you're planning your day's schedule, you may tell yourself it would be a good idea to leave ten minutes early to drop off the video you rented the night before. You will have planned how to go in the right direction to park in front of the store. How did you make these decisions? By using the left portion of your brain. It works to keep your life sensible, organized and on schedule. It's like a computer.

And then we have the right side of the brain. That portion of your brain comes into play when you work a jigsaw puzzle, look at a road map, design a new office, plan a room arrangement, solve a geometrical problem, or listen to musical selections on the stereo. The right half of your brain does not process information step-by-step like the left portion. Instead, it processes patterns of information. It plays host to our emotions. It has been called the intuitive side of the brain. It will link facts together and come up with a concept. It looks at the whole situation and, as though by magic, the solution appears. It's like a kaleidoscope.

The thinking pattern of the left side of your brain is positive, analytical, linear, explicit, sequential, verbal, concrete, rational and goal-oriented. The right side is intuitive, spontaneous, emotional, nonverbal, visual, artistic, playful, holistic and physical.

If you are right-side oriented and your spouse is left-side oriented, how will you communicate when it seems as though you speak different languages? And you probably do.

The Brain

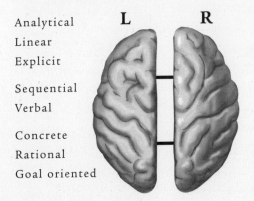

L	R
Analytical	Spontaneous
Linear	Intuitive
Explicit	Emotional
	(women excel)
Sequential	Nonverbal
Verbal	
Concrete	Visual, artistic
Rational	(women stronger)
Goal oriented	Holistic
	Spatial (men stronger)

Have you ever been in a class or even a church service where the speaker focused on dry, detailed facts? If he was inflexible, he was annoyed by interruptions to his train of thought. After each distraction he would return to the beginning and review. The speech was monotonous, delivered step-by-step with little emotional expression. If so, you were listening to a person who is an extreme—and I mean extreme—left-brain dominant.

If you listen to a speaker or someone in a conversation who rambles from topic to topic, relies on his or her own opinion and feelings, is easily led away from the point, leaves gaps in the presentation to give the conclusion, uses emotional language and hunches, then you're in the presence of the extreme right-brain dominant. The left side wants to know, "What's the bottom line?" The right side travels around the barn a few times to get there. As you'll see later, personality differences will also affect how a person responds.

When a man who is a highly proficient chemist also enjoys social activities and goes out dancing twice a week, which portion of his brain is he using for each task? He is using the left side for his work that must be careful, accurate and logical. When he's out dancing, he feels the steps by shifting to the right side of his brain. The chemist may be more comfortable using his left side, but he's able to make a switch for some right-brain activities. We continually shift back and forth between these two sides of the brain as we carry on our daily activities, although we will constantly reinforce our dominant side because it's easier to go that route than to break new ground by using the less dominant side.

Let's go back and look at men and women as children. Let's assume we have X-ray glasses so we can look into their brains. As you look inside, you may see a discrepancy between boys and girls.

In the brain there is a section that connects the left and right hemispheres. It is a bundle of nerves (the technical name is *corpus callosum*) and there are up to 40 percent more of these nerve connections in girls than in boys. This means that women are able to use both sides of the brain together at one time, whereas men have to switch from one side of the brain to the other, depending upon what they need to process. Women can enjoy more cross-talk between the sides because they use the brain holistically.

The extra connective tissue in girls is a reason why they develop language skills earlier than boys and will use many more words than their male counterparts. Do you know why boys often read more poorly than girls? It's the brain again. *The brain that will read better is the brain that can use both sides at once.* Interestingly, it is also easier to read the emotions on a person's face when you use both sides of your brain simultaneously.

A woman's brain has been developed to express and verbalize. This is why throughout adulthood she wants to "talk about it." A man's brain has been geared to develop his spatial skills. This is why throughout his life he wants to "do something about it." So a woman is usually quicker to talk about her feelings, while a man wants to act quickly to *do* something about it.

These differences are where the conflicts arise (and probably always will). A woman will say, "Let's sit down and talk this through." Meanwhile, the man is straining at the bit to get it fixed and get on with life! *Remember: Neither response is wrong and neither is better than the other.*

In studies at the University of Pennsylvania, brainscan equipment has been used to generate computer photographs of brains in use. The scans look almost like maps. The equipment photographs brain activity and manifests it in different colors, with each color showing a different degree of intense cortical activity.

When a man and woman are hooked up to the equipment, they are both asked to do a spatial task, such as figuring out how two objects fit together. If you looked at a computer screen that depicts the activity in the woman's brain, you would see that the color and intensity on both sides are pretty equal. But something happens to the man's brain. The right side lights up with various colors that reflect a high degree of right-brain activity. Much less of the left hemisphere lights up.

On the other hand, when verbal skills are tested, watch out! Then you would see that the man uses much less of his brain when compared to the scan of the woman's, which now shows a high intensity of activity in her left hemisphere! Recently in a seminar I had opportunity to see such pictures. A brainscan on a woman showed activity on both sides of the brain when the woman was talking. But when the man was talking, the brain scan indicated activity on only one side of the brain—the left side.

The findings of this research indicate that a woman's brain is at work in more sections than the man's almost all the time. It's as if both hemispheres are always on call, whereas in a man's brain one hemisphere at a time is on call.

Think of it like this: If there is a task to do, a man's brain turns on. When the task is completed, the brain turns off. But a woman's brain is always on. It's true that parts of a man's brain are always on, too, but when the two brains are compared in their downtime or inactive time, the difference between the portion of the woman's brain that is always on and that of a man's is quite pronounced.[4]

There are other results of the fact that women have more and thicker nerve connectors between the two sides of the brain.

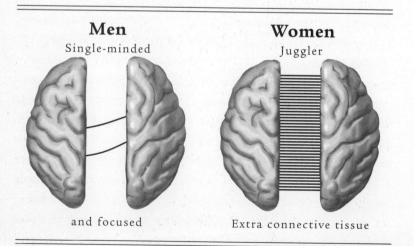

Men
Single-minded

Women
Juggler

and focused

Extra connective tissue

Women can tune in to everything going on around them. A woman may handle five hectic work activities at one time while a male coworker is reading a report, totally oblivious to the various problems going on around him. She can juggle more items but can be distracted more easily. He can focus on one task better but can lose sight of other aspects. He has to stop one activity in order to attend to another.

The result of this difference causes women to be more perceptive than men about people. Women have a greater ability to pick up feelings and sense the difference between what people say and what they mean. Women's intuition has a physical basis. A woman's brain is like a computer that can integrate reason and intuition.

This drives some men crazy. There are numerous stories about the wife who says to her husband, speaking about someone else, that she thinks there is a problem or that something is going on. The husband wants to know how she knows . . . where are the facts? The wife then says she doesn't have any facts. She just senses it. The husband tells her she doesn't know what she's talking about. But a week later, when he finds out she was right, he's amazed and even more puzzled.

It could be that women pick up more information than men do because their sensitivities, such as hearing, eyesight, sense of taste and smell are usually more heightened than a man's.

The hearing difference is noted even in childhood. Men in general hear in one ear better than in the other. Females in general hear more data and hear equally well in both ears. All the way through life, males hear less than females, which creates profound problems in relationships. It's been noted that boys from a very early age ignore voices, even parents' voices, more than girls do. Why? In some of these cases the boys are simply not hearing. They are also poorer than girls at picking out background noises. Boys, quite simply, hear less background noise and differentiate less. This is one of the reasons that parents and anyone around a boy often report having to speak more loudly to the boy than to a girl.[5]

So what does this difference mean? It's the main reason that men are fixers—that they are task-oriented and not as able to do several things at once. They need to focus on one thing at a time.

An interesting sidelight of this difference is that because men tend to operate only from one side of the brain at any given time, they find it easier to identify left from right. A large number of women find it difficult to tell their left hand from their right without looking at it first.

If you were able to watch a woman brush her teeth, you might see her doing two tasks at once that took opposite movements to pull off—brushing her teeth with up and down strokes while she wiped down the sink countertop using circular motions. You probably wouldn't see a man do that. When he brushes his teeth, he plants his feet right in front of the sink a foot apart, bends over the sink and often moves his head back and forth against the brush. It's our brain differences that do this.

When a man takes on a task at home, such as cleaning the garage or working in the yard, to him it's a single-focus task, *not a fellowship time.* If his wife wants to work with him, she usually wants to carry on a conversation at the same time. To him this may seem like an interruption, an invasion of his space, a distraction. And he reacts strongly to it.

Have you ever noticed a man's sentences as compared to a woman's? They are usually shorter and more structured. When you analyze the sentence it has a simple opening, a central point and a conclusion. (There are exceptions to this, based on personality differences.)

For most men, if you present several different ideas to at him at once, you'll lose him. This is so important for women to understand, in both the business world and in working at church. If a woman wants what she is saying to register with a man, give him one clear thought at a time. If a man or woman is speaking to a mixed group, it's better to use the male pattern of presenting ideas. Otherwise, if you ramble or present several different tracks at once, the men may lose interest.[6]

WHEN DIFFERENCES COLLIDE

Generally speaking, when it comes to approaching and solving problems, women use both sides of the brain and are able to create an overview. Men tend to break down problems into pieces in order to come up with a solution. A man tends to go through steps 1, 2, 3 and 4 to come up with a solution. He uses a linear approach. A woman tends to go through steps 1, 3, 2, 5 and 4 and come up to the same conclusion. If she arrives there before the man does, he probably won't accept her correct answer because he hasn't completed steps 1, 2, 3 and 4 yet. He's not ready for her answer.

When that happens a woman tends to feel that her coworker isn't listening. He is listening, but he's not ready yet to respond. She complains, "It's obvious, why can't you see it?" He can't see it because that's not the way he thinks.

A man says of a woman's seemingly random approach, "Just take it one step at a time. You can't approach it that way." But she can. Neither approach is wrong—just different. Can you imagine what a man and woman could accomplish if they learned to use each other's creativity and strength?[7]

Men like structure. Men like to put things in order. They like to regulate, organize, enumerate (men love to talk about numbers and statistics) and fit things into rules and patterns. It's not unusual for a man to take the time to put his CDs and videos in alphabetical order, to figure out how long it takes to walk two miles or drive 85 miles to his favorite fishing hole. Ever wonder why some men have a set routine on Saturday? Maybe the plan is to wash the car, mow the lawn, trim the roses and take a nap. And he always does it at the same time and in the same order.[8] This plan provides structure and conserves energy. Keep the word *energy* in mind, for it's a source of contention between men and women.

Men See One Tree at a Time

The way in which men use their brains is *exclusive*. (Some women refer to it as tunnel vision!) It can exclude everything except what he is focusing on. It shuts out other possibilities. And men exert an abundance of energy to stay in this position. Most men like to know exactly where they are and what they are doing at a given point in time. It's a way to stay in control.

When a man's attention is locked onto the computer or a financial printout, he is in his exclusive mindset. If a woman chooses this time to talk to him about the office party, it feels like interference or intrusion to him. *For him it's an energy leak.* He hopes it will leave! When he does exert energy to shift from whatever he was doing to concentrate on her questions, he may be upset because of the energy expenditure. He has to change his focus and shift it elsewhere because he can't handle both issues at once.

She feels he's inconsiderate for not listening or caring and he feels she's inconsiderate because of the intrusion. Actually, neither is inconsiderate. They just don't understand the gender difference. If they did, they could each learn to respond differently.

Women See a Forest

Women are *inclusive* and can jump in and out of different topics. There's no energy drain for them. A woman actually picks up energy by entering into new experiences or changes. She is able to see the situation and beyond. She sees and responds to life like a camera with a wide-angle lens, whereas a man's camera has a highly focused microscope lens. He sees the tree in great detail;

she sees the tree, but she also sees the grove and its potential. A woman's expectation of a man's perceptual ability should be tempered with this knowledge.[9]

Remember, there will be exceptions to what is said here. Some men and women will be just the opposite. My wife and I are exceptions. I tend to be the juggler and she is more single-minded. It also appears that personality preference (which is discussed in later chapters) has a modifying effect on some of these characteristics.

Here's another issue: Since a man focuses on one thing at a time and a woman can handle several things at a time, if she's doing two or three things while talking to him, he feels that she's not paying attention to him. If she were interested, she would look at him with 100 percent attention. Here's a choice example that I've heard expressed in a similar way many times:

> Men also can't understand how women can leave the theater or the living room during the most important part of a movie and go to the bathroom. A man will hold it! He has his priorities. He also has a larger bladder! On the other hand, the woman's "inclusive" mode gives her a sense of what's going on in the film, and she can still "watch" the film while she's in the bathroom. If the man is not physically watching the movie, he misses out. Even though she may not have caught all the details, she doesn't have a sense of missing anything.[10]

Men and Women Handle Feelings Differently

This brings us to a question you have probably heard again and again over the years: *Why can't a man access feelings like a woman can?* The answer is that men have three strikes against them when it comes to feelings.

One, they're wired differently.

Two, they're raised to be emotionally handicapped. They're given neither the encouragement nor training to learn to understand a wide range of feelings, nor to develop a vocabulary to express them. By the way, men and women do not have different emotions. God created all of us as emotional beings. But the way emotions are dealt with and expressed are often different.

Three, the way women attempt to get to a man's feelings often becomes counterproductive. Pressuring, or even asking a man, "How do you feel?" usually doesn't work.

Again, we must look at the brain to see why men and women have to deal with their feelings differently.

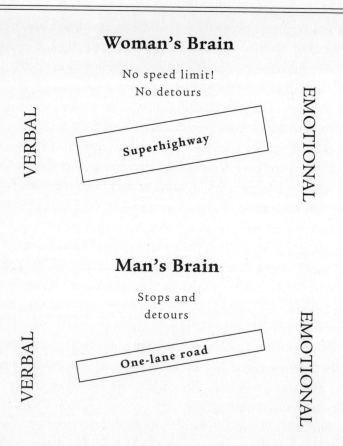

Woman's Brain

No speed limit!
No detours

VERBAL

Superhighway

EMOTIONAL

Man's Brain

Stops and
detours

VERBAL

One-lane road

EMOTIONAL

A woman has an immense number of neuroconnectors between her feelings and the broadcasting studio in her brain. She has an expressway that runs between her feelings and her speech. And because her brain is basically on all the time, it's very easy for her to share these feelings.

Remember that a man's brain has fewer nerve connectors between its right and left sides. No wonder, then, that he often has more of a struggle than a woman in expressing feelings. He doesn't have an expressway between feelings and the broadcasting area of the brain, but more of a one-way street.[11]

This is why it's not easy for a man to share. If he attempts to put his feelings into words, he must take a prior step called *thought*. He has to ask, "Now, I'm feeling something. What is it? All right, that's what it is." Once he discovers his feelings, he must analyze them and decide what he can do about them.

Remember that a man's brain is a problem-solving brain. He is wired to have delayed reactions. When an emotional event occurs, is he ready yet to express his feelings? No. He needs to move over to the left side of his brain and collect the words to express his feelings. That stops many men from expressing emotions; they are vocabulary-deficient for the most part.

It's not all their fault. Parents, teachers and society as a whole fail to provide much help in teaching men the vocabulary of feelings or the ability to paint word pictures to describe their feelings. The man shares what he's able to share, and when new feelings arise it's back to the drawing board to start the process all over again.

So remember this difference: *A man has to think about his feelings before he can share them. A woman can feel, talk and think at the same time.*[12]

To fine-tune this concept, let's consider the sequential difference in how a woman and a man process feelings. When a woman is upset, what does she do first? She talks about it. As she talks she is able to think about what she's saying and feeling.

The end result is that she figures it out—usually by herself. She begins with feelings, then moves to talking and then to thinking.

Eventually she develops the ability to do all three at the same time:

Feeling—————————————*Talking*———————————————Thinking

Because a woman problem-solves out loud, most men either think they've caused the problem or that the woman wants them to solve the problem. It's possible that he *could* fix it, but only if she requests a solution. Most women just want a man to listen and reflect the fact that he has heard what she's saying.

If a man encourages a woman to express her negative feelings in any situation, she soon lets go of them and can remember and identify the positives. This is what women tend to do—talk about negatives out loud, which helps them to discover the positives. When a woman expresses these negatives in a meeting at work or church, the men usually jump in to fix, correct, point out that it's not so bad or defend. Actually all of that is a waste of time.

Now, a man is not going to deal with his feelings in the same sequence as a woman. Often his feelings develop; then he moves to action and then to thinking. When an upset occurs, a man's immediate response is to do something about it; and that helps him think it through. In time, he learns to feel, *act* and think at the same time:

Feeling——————————————— *Acting* ——————————————Thinking

You will notice that *talking* to resolve the problem isn't part of the formula for men. Communication is more significant for a woman, while action is more significant for a man.[13]

When a woman understands this, she doesn't have to be surprised when it occurs. She can accept this sequence of processing feelings and even encourage the man to respond in this way. She can also adapt some of her typical responses to more nearly match his.

Keep in mind that each side of the brain has, as it were, its own language. If a man is stronger in his left brain function (in other words, if he's left-brain dominant), his language is going to be concerned with facts. It will tend to be logical and precise, as well as black and white.

Notes

1. Judith Tingley, *Genderflex*™: *Men and Women Speaking Each Other's Language at Work* (New York: Amacon, 1993), pp. 9-10, adapted.
2. Ibid., p. 5.
3. Michael McGill, *The McGill Report on Male Intimacy* (San Francisco: Harper and Row, 1985), p. 74.
4. Michael Gurian, *The Wonder of Boys* (New York: G. P. Putnam, 1996), pp. 11-15, adapted.
5. Ibid., pp. 16, 17, adapted.
6. Barbara and Allan Pease, *Why Men Don't Listen and Women Can't Read Maps* (New York, Welcome Rain Publishers, 2000), p. 84, adapted.
7. Joe Tanenbaum, *Male and Female Realities* (San Marcos, CA: Robert Erdmann Publishing, 1990), pp. 96, 97, adapted.
8. Josh Shapiro, M.D., *Men, A Translation for Women* (New York: Avon Books, 1992), pp. 71ff, adapted.
9. Tanenbaum, *Male and Female Realities,* pp. 40, 82, adapted. See also Jacquelyn Wonder and Pricilla Donavan, *Whole Brain Thinking* (New York: William Morrow and Company, 1984), pp. 18ff, adapted.
10. Tanenbaum, p. 90.
11. Gurian, *The Wonder of Boys,* p. 23, adapted.
12. John Gray, *What Your Mother Couldn't Tell You and Your Father Didn't Know* (New York: HarperCollins, 1994), p. 90, adapted; for more information on the subject of brain differences of men and women, see Joe Tanenbaum, *Male and Female Realities,* chaps. 4-6; John Gray, *Mars and Venus Together Forever,* and his even more popular *Men Are from Mars, Women Are from Venus* (New York:HarperCollins, 1992).
13. Gray, *What Your Mother Couldn't Tell You and Your Father Didn't Know*, pp. 90, 91, adapted.

CHAPTER 10

LEARNING TO SPEAK EACH OTHER'S LANGUAGE

At work I seem to connect better with the other men when I discuss something.
When I talk with some of the women in the group, well, we're discussing the
same topic, but I wonder if we're really on the same page.

If left-brained men and right-brained women are ever to communicate across their natural gender gap, they must learn to
understand and use each other's language style to some extent.
In other words, they must become bilingual!

The differences between the brain function preferences in
men and women, discussed in chapter 9, mean that when men
and women communicate (or attempt to!) they have different purposes in mind. Women speak and hear a language of
connection and intimacy, whereas a man tends to speak and

hear a language of status and independence.

The way men speak is *report*-talk. They like to express knowledge and skills. They use talking as a way to get and keep attention.

Women's speech is *rapport*-talk. It's their way of establishing connection and negotiating relationships.

So what you have is not really a difference of dialects within the same language, but actually cross-cultural communication. It's been said that men and women speak different *genderlects*.[1]

One of the other sources of miscommunication in cross-gender communication is the fact that men and women use different dictionaries. They define the same word differently. It helps if they take the position that they can't assume they know what the other person means by a word and they need to ask for clarification. If this were to happen, men and women would understand each other to a greater degree.

Let's consider a hypothetical situation to illustrate becoming "bilingual." Let's assume that you have met a family from another country while they are traveling in the United States. You spend some time showing them around and they invite you and your family to come visit them. You accept the invitation. But then it dawns on you that you're not even sure where their home is, and you know nothing about its culture, customs or language. You want to get the most out of your visit. You want to enjoy this new country and be respectful of this family's traditions.

In an effort to do this, you acquire books and tapes to help you understand your new friends. Many people would even spend time learning the other culture's language. It's true, you wouldn't learn all you needed to know beforehand, but with an open learning attitude, you would learn. If you do make a cultural mistake while visiting your new friends, you would probably apologize and attempt to learn the proper response. The number of possible mistakes will have been greatly reduced because of your willingness to learn and become flexible.

If you follow this same approach at church and at work by learning about different learning styles and gender and personality differences, and you look at the problems as cultural misunderstandings, you can learn to get along better with the other sex.

> The male-female difference represents the biggest culture gap that exists. If you can learn the skills and attitudes to bridge the gender differences in communication, you will have mastered what it takes to communicate and negotiate *with* almost anyone *about* almost anything.[2]

A new word, "genderflex," has been coined for this situation. It's not in the dictionary yet, but it will be. The word means to temporarily use communication patterns typical of the other gender in order to connect with them and increase the potential for influence and rapport.[3]

A new word, "genderflex," is not in the dictionary yet, but it will be. It means to temporarily use communication patterns typical of the opposite gender in order to connect and also increase the potential for influence.

This is an adaptive approach to communication designed to improve relationships and performance. *It's not a change in personality, lifestyle or values.* It's an adaptation that will actually create greater flexibility and growth among those practicing it. You choose to communicate in the patterns of the other gender to accomplish a goal. You simply adopt the characteristics of the opposite gender that are related to style, content and structure of communication. You're not becoming like the other gender, you are showing that you understand how they communicate.

UNDERSTANDING EACH OTHER'S LANGUAGE

Expressers and Resolvers

Genderflex talk will reflect the reality that women tend to speak the language of *expressers* and men tend to speak the language of *resolvers*. What happens in communication between men and women at the office, at board and company meetings and at church is the same as communication interaction in marriage. The lack of understanding of these differences creates tension and misunderstandings again and again.

So often when a woman talks, she's doing it just to express. She's sharing to communicate. It's her way of interacting with the world. She's not looking for a solution or an answer; she just wants to express.

Because this is true most of the time, a problem can arise when a woman does want an answer or a solution. Jim voiced a common reaction among men: "Sometimes she does want a solution, but I've learned to back off. For a long time I'd give a solution and that's not what she wanted! I'm not a mind reader." There will be times when a woman doesn't even know she needs an answer until she talks about it for a while. It helps if a man realizes that most women cannot tell them in advance whether they need or want an answer. If men would realize this and be patient, there would be a greater level of harmony.

It would also help if women remembered that men usually talk for the purpose of resolving something. Even if a man knows that a woman just needs to talk for the purpose of talking through an issue and isn't looking for a solution, yet she doesn't inform the man, he will try to fix the problem. If a woman is offended by this, the man may be offended by her response, and the tension builds in the office.

Think about a conference-room setting or a church meeting. Who designs most of these meetings? In most cases, men. There are planning meetings, informational meetings and brainstorming meetings. Each has a purpose with its own set of rules.[4]

One writer described a man's way of communicating as a three-stage process. First a man mulls, then he stores and then he communicates. Men tend to have a back burner they put a problem or situation on when it occurs. Mulling occurs on the back burner and it doesn't take much energy. Most men want to delay and see if a problem can be resolved or go away with as little energy output as possible. Some men can mull for weeks and usually do not communicate during this time. It would be a waste of time to communicate if the problem can be resolved on its own. If mulling doesn't work, a man moves on to the next stage.

Often when a man is sitting there apparently doing nothing, just looking into space or staring out the window, he actually is doing something. More likely than not he's having a conversation with himself. Many men engage in silent talk. They don't have to fill the silence with audible words. One of my closest friends is this way. I'm the talker; he is not. We can sit in the boat fishing side by side and not say a word for 15 minutes, but we're both probably carrying on a conversation in our heads.

Keep in mind that most men prefer to retreat into silence when there's a problem. A man does this to hold a conversation with himself and find a solution. If he's interrupted during this time, he's not a happy camper. He wants to be left alone. The problem is that most men don't bother to say, "I want to think about this issue for a while by myself. That really helps me find a solution. And when I do I'll be sure to let you know." If men would do this at work and at home, women would give a greater level of acceptance to their seeming noncommunication.

Can you imagine a situation at church or at work in which the pressure exerted on a man by others didn't allow for any time to mull something over? Even in a simple argument or disagreement, some men need time to think things over before responding. If he doesn't get the time, or he's pressured by too much verbiage, he'll become loud and/or angry. This is a typical response. And this is more likely to happen when his communication skills are minimal.

Most women do not need to mull things over (unless they are introverts), but men do not always understand this. They think, "If I need to mull it over, so does she." All this does is delay the communication process.

Because men talk to fix and women to express, their goals and purposes for communication are different. That also makes their styles of communication different.

Many men see communication as another sporting event. Do you view communicating as something to win, lose or draw? Many men do. That's why when a conversation is over, for a man it's really over. "If we finished talking about it, why go back and rehash it again?" This is why men become irritated when a woman wants to talk about something again.

Women communicate to understand others and to let others understand them. This is why the same subject can be brought up and rehearsed, analyzed and dissected time and time again. Each time results in greater understanding.

The problem isn't the content of the communication, it's the style. It's the fact that each gender just keeps talking to the other according to their own gender's style. And so neither one really gets through to the other. When this happens, neither one looks forward to talking.[5]

The solution is simple. Learn to speak one another's language. How do you do that?

Favorite Topics of Conversation

Most studies show there is a major difference in what men and women talk about. The content is different. Even if men and women are on the same topic they will probably have a different focus. Men generally talk about money, sports and business. They talk to report and gain information. Women talk to relate, so they usually talk about people, relationships and feelings. There's also a difference in their style of talking. Both of these issues—content and style—create the most conflict between men and women, whether at home, at work or in a church-work setting.

Men, it is okay to continue to talk about what you do, whether it's sports, hobbies, business or money. And it's okay to continue to use your style. That's all right. It's good. But remember the principle of this book: Those who have the flexibility to adapt and speak another's language will get along better with the largest group of people and have the most influence. In your conversation with women, add the topics of people, relationships and feelings. Use stories, word pictures and learn to use a feeling vocabulary. Become comfortable with listening and reflecting back what you're hearing. Give feedback to show that you not only heard, but you also understood. And one more thing: Go easy on your style of humor.[6]

Women, continue to talk about people, relationships and feelings. Don't give up the relating talk. You know a lot about these subjects. But in talking with a man, just keep it brief and specific and men will listen better. If you're talking with a man, ask yourself, "Does he need to hear all this or even want to hear it?" It's better to give a very brief response and have a man ask for more detail (which will happen) than to have him sit there and wonder *When will it end?* When you talk with a man, keep your remarks clear, specific and bottom line.

It will also help to add sports, money and business to the content of your conversations. You don't have to become an expert on these subjects, but with a little reading or listening you can pick up enough information to be conversant. By asking insightful questions of men, you can let them build your level of knowledge in these areas.

When I operated a large counseling center, I appreciated the women on staff who would bring in cartoons or use humor. Some could exchange witty comments as well as the men. Humor is essential for both men and women as they learn to speak each other's language.[7]

Expanders and Condensers

A simple example and variation of the *expresser* and *resolver* is that typically most women are *expanders* and most men are *condensers* in the content of what they share. That is, women tend to give much more detail and include feelings when they share, whereas men tend to give bottom-line, factual information.

Many women want to share details since they're important to her and are needed in many cases. It's not so much the sharing of details between a man and a woman that's the problem, it's the packaging. Unless a man sees the details as connected to the point, they aren't that important to him. Often women are sharing an experience. I've seen it work well when a woman in a meeting states, "Let me give you some background to help put this in perspective," or "Would you like the bottom line first or the information that will make this come alive first?"[8]

To really speak genderflex language, even if a woman is talking about interpersonal situations, she would use more factual descriptions that focus on identifying a problem or a solution rather than an abundance of details or feelings. And a man would not give just "bottom-line" facts but descriptive details with an emphasis on the interpersonal.[9]

It's true that when men work together they want to deal with the facts first. And men will look outside of themselves to discover the cause of a problem, while women look inside. When a man looks outside of himself, some may interpret this as looking for someone else to blame. For instance, when he says, "How did that happen?" or "Who did that?" it can be interpreted as blame. Men do tend to look around for a person to be the source of the problem and then attempt to fix that person.

Women tend to look within themselves for the source of the problem: "Did I do something to create this problem?" Some women will even volunteer that they might have caused the problem. How would a man respond to this suggestion? Would he tend to discuss it or look for other causes? Probably not. He's more likely to factually respond with, "All right, let's fix it." To a woman this doesn't sound like teamwork, and she might feel offended.

A man's view of teamwork is different from a woman's. It's more like, "All right. Here's what needs to be done. Jim, you do this task. John, you take over this one and I'll work on this phase." They work side by side with little interaction and they get it done.

Differences between men and women occur not because of the topic being discussed but because of the way communication is delivered as well as the purpose of the conversation.

Women tend to take a different approach. They want to talk the process through and establish a team purpose. Men work independently, whereas a group of women are interdependent.

Can you see the potential for conflict if you have a group of men and women on the same church or business board or committee? What defines teamwork for one gender may not be the same for the other. Each gender could learn some things from one another, such as:

Men could state out loud that they aren't blaming others when looking for a solution and then perhaps could look inside themselves for their contribution to a problem. They could also learn to interact more with the women in the group by letting them know what they're thinking, as well as their intentions.

Women could learn to identify team members' functions and realize that they're still working as a team even when there isn't a lot of interaction. And perhaps they could learn not to be so quick to think of themselves as contributors to a problem but to balance this with outside factors.

And it's even more helpful when each gender understands that each has a different approach to problem solving and that neither approach is wrong.[10]

THE PURPOSES BEHIND TALK

Topics of conversation vary between men and women. One major study indicates that both men and women talk about work, movies and television. But women talk more about relationship issues, families, health and reproduction, weight, eating and clothing. Men talk more about sports, current events and music.

Differences between men and women occur not because of the topic being discussed but because of the way in which the communication is delivered, as well as the purpose of the conversation.

The purpose of men's conversation with other men is for the freedom they feel, as well as camaraderie. Men like *not* having to be careful about what they say. This is one of the things men enjoy most about talking with other men. Men also like fast-paced interaction, the use of a lot of humor and talking about practical things.

Women enjoy talking with other women for some of the same reasons—the ease of it and the fellowship. But for the woman this means empathy and understanding. Sensitivity to emotions is a critical ingredient of their conversations with other women. Women are much more likely to call another woman *just to talk,* whereas men like to have a purpose and an agenda when they converse.

Men and women have different expectations of one another when they talk. Men expect women to converse with them in the same way as other men—staying surface level, unemotional, fast-paced, practical and fun. Women expect something else from men—less bottom-line conversation and a show of interest in personal and emotional issues. Women tend to expect that they can be open in their conversations with men, but a man's responses are usually all wrong for her. A direct and practical response does not meet a woman's empathetic needs. When a man tries to fix a problem, a woman interprets it as rejection. This misunderstanding doesn't just occur at home; it happens in church situations and especially in the workplace.[11]

How do these insights affect the way we communicate with the opposite sex? Consider the following statements:

Go and get some donuts and coffee for our meeting.

Could you get some donuts and coffee for our meeting?

Would you please get donuts and coffee for our meeting?

Do you think we should have donuts and coffee for our meeting?

Wouldn't it be super to have donuts and coffee for our meeting?

Would you like to have donuts and coffee for our meeting?

There are direct and indirect approaches here. Who is most likely to use either type? If you said men for the first three and women for the last three, you are correct. Men are direct in what they say, whereas women tend to be indirect. Men effectively use the direct style in business, but this style doesn't always work in interpersonal relationships.

Women tend to be indirect or even hint about something. Indirect speech is great for building rapport or relationships. Phrases like "kind of" and "sort of" are examples of indirect speech, and women can easily pick up the meaning of them. However, men do not pick up on hints very well. A man translates a woman's words literally and can miss the meaning, since he uses communication as a way to explain facts and information. Therefore, it's best when talking with a man to avoid beating around the bush.

Men are able to communicate well with women if they remind themselves to whom they are speaking and what kind of words communicate best. For example, with a woman, a man needs to ask more questions, reflect what he thinks he has heard, avoid volunteering solutions right away and realize that there could be more meaning to a statement than it appears. A man should not respond to a statement unless he gets some clarification. It helps if a man says to himself, "I need to use her dictionary, not mine." And he will probably feel less defensive. When both genders try to understand the way the opposite gender thinks and processes emotion, conflict drops way off.[12]

It works! I've seen it happen! And once again, this goes back to the principle that those who exercise the greatest flexibility will connect with more people and get along better.

Transcribing a Man's Shorthand

Men tend to use a form of verbal shorthand that other men find acceptable but most women do not. These statements are often used when men want space or some silent acceptance. You've probably used these words (if you're a man) or heard them (if you're a woman). Do they sound familiar?

"I'm OK" or "It's OK."

"Fine" or "It's fine."

"It's no big deal."

"No problem."

What do these words mean? "OK" usually means, "I can handle what's going on." If a man would just verbalize these extra six words and add, "I don't need any assistance, but thanks for asking," it would do wonders to advance communication between the sexes.

We all joke about men saying, "Fine." But it's true, we do use this word a lot. It means, "I can handle this situation," "I feel on top of the situation," "I know what to do," or "I really don't need any help, but if I do I'll ask you." It's all right to say "fine," but we need to add the rest of the story and then it really will be *fine*.

If a man doesn't expand the comment, "It's no big deal," a woman could interpret it as, "You're making a big deal out of something that isn't a big deal. Don't overreact." This won't happen if the man adds some commentary like, "I know how to make this work out. It helps me more if we don't talk any more about this or dwell on it. I understand your concern and I can see what I did. I do want to resolve this."

"No problem" usually means, "I can solve this issue," or "It's not a problem for me to tackle this. In fact, I'd like to take care of this." Most women would feel quite satisfied to hear a response like this. It also helps if a woman learns to say, "Fine," "No problem," and "It's no big deal." When a man hears phrases like this, he tends to listen more.[13]

The Importance of Humor

In Ecclesiastes 3:4, it states, "There is . . . a time to laugh." Laughter is a gift from God. It facilitates many things, from giving people a break from the heaviness of life to serving as a way to break the ice in a tense committee meeting.

But there are differences in humor. What is funny to one person may not be to another. I use a lot of humor in my seminars. Many of the jokes and sayings are goofs and misquotes we can all identify with. Some have to do with gender differences. One is a wild and funny drawing of the differences between the male and female brain; another is a listing of how a dog is a better companion than a man or woman. These are a light and humorous means of looking at the gender differences we're all familiar with.

Men use humor in any work situation to bond and build a team. It's one of the ways they relieve stress. Practical jokes and comments at the expense of another man are typical behavior. One woman, overhearing the exchange of two men, said, "I thought they liked each other. But judging from the way they put one another down and some of their comments . . . I wonder."

The reason men respond in this way is because they *do* like one another. Their closeness and comfort with each other lets them talk this way. Men use teasing and roasting, and some have perfected it to a fine art. I've had many pranks pulled on me and I've done the same to my seven close male friends. The fact that they take the time, the thought, the energy and the creativity to pull what they do shows that we have a strong connection.

If a man responds to a woman coworker or friend with the same form of humor, well, it's like a death wish, since she'll probably be offended and it shows he doesn't understand male-female differences.

Women tend to take a man's humorous comments personally. Most of the time these comments are not serious or personal.

I've found that many men just don't know how to interact in a humorous way. Men can tease about hair, body shape, clothes and coordination with other men, but this is off-limits with a woman.

Many women have learned to respond with appropriate comebacks to the aggressive humor of men. These are the women who interact the best in the workplace. But if a woman responds with a counterattack that is offensive, the man wonders what's going on.

Women's humor tends to use self-ridicule, probably because of a tendency to introspection. It helps if women who work with men can learn a man's more teasing style. It's an important skill for both church and the workplace. It would also be helpful for men who work with women to consider picking up on a woman's style of humor.[14]

WHO ADJUSTS TO WHOM?

Over the years it seems the emphasis has been upon women making the adjustments in order to get along with men. Today the emphasis is on both genders learning to adapt. For men to adapt to women in a business setting isn't something they're used to doing. But they're capable of doing it and, fortunately, many are making the effort. If both men and women learn to be adaptive communicators in the workplace, not only will they get along better but the productivity and efficiency will also be increased.

Adaptive communication means language harmony, or learning to speak the other person's language. Suzette Elgin, in her book *The Last Word on the Gentle Art of Verbal Self-Defense*, said, "There are few communication strategies more guaranteed to fail than making adjustments based upon nothing but your personal determination to talk in a particular way *no matter what happens*."[15] You have to make your adjustments based upon how the other person responds to what you say.[16]

Keep in mind that you will find exceptions to these male-female styles. Some men will express themselves in a style easily understood by women, and some women will express themselves in a style easily understood by men. This is probably due to the influence of personality variation.

More Characteristics of Male-Female Talk

By the way, are you aware that men talk more than women? It's true! There hasn't been a single study that gives any evidence that women talk more than men, but there are numerous studies showing that men talk more than women.[17]

It's also true that women talk much more than men *on the subjects of people, feelings and relationships,* just as men talk more than women on *their* preferred content.

Many men will say they prefer talking to women rather than to men because women are better at conversation. What women are actually better at is listening and the art of supporting the other person's conversational efforts, which include encouraging them to go on, enabling them to explain fully and reinforcing their conversational efforts with smiles, head nods, good eye contact and other indications of attentiveness.

Certain words and categories of words appear much more frequently in women's speech than in men's. Adverbs denoting intensity (such as "awfully," "terribly," "pretty," "quite," "so," and the adjectives "charming," "lovely," "adorable," "divine," "cute" and "sweet") are more common in a woman's conversation.

Women also have a much more extensive vocabulary for colors than men. Words for colors like "taupe," "beige," "mauve," "lavender" and "violet" are not common in men's speech. Males are not expected to discuss the "lovely mauve drapes" in the conference room or the "streaks of lavender" in the sunset.

Creating Closeness or Simply Exchanging Information?

Men and women have been taught to use language differently. For women, speech communication is basically for social relationships. Women have been raised to use communication as a mechanism for creating bonds. Men, on the other hand, have been encouraged to communicate primarily to exchange information.

Most men tend to feel more comfortable speaking in public than in private, intimate conversations. With most women it's just the opposite. Women enjoy private one-on-one conversations because they are more personal and they build relationships. For most men, conversation is used to gain status, to solve problems and negotiate, to get attention and even to keep their independence.[18]

Wording Your Requests to Get the Right Response

Communicating for change involves making requests. But too often requests sound like demands. When a man or a woman makes a request, timing is critical. For example, if a man asks for something when a woman is in the midst of some project, he can't expect an immediate response. And perhaps he doesn't, but the woman may interpret the request as an expectation for immediate response. It would be helpful to add, "I'm not asking for it or needing it right now; I just want to know if . . ." or "Could you get this to me by tomorrow?"

If a woman sees a man just about to do a task, it's best not to ask him to do *what he is obviously going to do*. And if he's focused on some project, it's better to wait before requesting the next task, or leave him a note.

What happens in a work setting if a woman begins to give a man advice before he asks for it? He probably won't accept her words since he hasn't asked for advice or worked on the problem yet. When advice comes prematurely, he sees it as an insult. Even if the advice is good, he will reject it.

Even worse than premature advice is a premature suggestion to call in an expert. To many men, that's like saying, "You don't have the ability to do it. Let's get someone who can." A man thinks you're saying he's incompetent. One of the most disarming responses a woman can make when she's bringing up a problem is to say, "This isn't your fault" or "If it sounds like I'm saying it's your fault, I'm not. No one is being blamed." This has helped many a male-female interaction.[19]

One of the gunpowder phrases that women can avoid saying to men is, "You don't understand." These words are deadly. Even if the man is interrupting, correcting or trying to use solutions, don't say it. To a man, the phrase "You don't understand" sounds like criticism and doesn't make any sense to him. He wants to prove he does understand. There is an alternative phrase that John Gray has suggested, and it works: "Let me try saying this in another way." These words convey the same meaning as "You don't understand," but in a noncritical way.[20]

By now you probably have a better understanding of the basic gender differences when it comes to talk interaction. You also have a better understanding of yourself and why some of your conversations with the opposite sex have been less than successful. The question now is, What will you do differently in order to communicate better? The next step is up to you.

Just remember, if you apply the principle of genderflex, your interactions at your place of employment, at church or in the context of any other type of male-female work situation will develop into meaningful and successful communication.

Notes

1. Deborah Tannen, Ph.D., *You Just Don't Understand* (New York: Morrow Publishing, 1990), pp. 42, 77, adapted.
2. George Simons, *Transcultural Leadership, Empowering the Diverse Work Force* (Houston, TX: Gulf Publishing, 1993).
3. Judith C. Tingley, Ph.D., *Genderflex™: Men and Women Speaking Each Other's Language at Work* (New York: Amacon, 1993), p. 16, adapted.

4. Joe Tanenbaum, *Male and Female Realities* (San Marcos, CA: Robert Erdmann Publishers, 1990), pp. 122-124, adapted.

5. Tingley, *Genderflex™*, pp. 27-33, adapted.

6. Ibid., pp. 80-87, adapted.

7. Ibid., pp. 56-62, adapted.

8. John Gray, *Mars and Venus Together Forever* (New York: HarperCollins, 1994), pp. 143, 144, adapted.

9. Tingley, *Genderflex™*, p. 19, adapted.

10. Tanenbaum, *Male and Female Realities,* pp. 140, 141, adapted.

11. Ibid., pp. 112-115, adapted.

12. Barbara and Allan Pease, *Why Men Don't Listen and Women Can't Read Maps* (New York: Welcome Rain Publishers, 2000), pp. 89-91, adapted.

13. John Gray, Ph.D., *Men Are from Mars, Women Are from Venus* (New York: HarperCollins, 1992), pp. 72-75, adapted.

14. Tanenbaum, pp. 153-159, adapted.

15. Suzette Haden Elgin, *The Last Word on the Gentle Art of Verbal Self-Defense* (New York: Prentice Hall, 1989).

16. Tingley, *Genderflex™*, pp. 14, 15, adapted.

17. Ibid., p. 29, adapted.

18. Tannen, *You Just Don't Understand*, p. 77, adapted.

19. Gray, *Men Are from Mars, Women Are from Venus*, pp. 83, 88, adapted.

20. Gray, *Mars and Venus Together Forever*, pp. 131, 132, adapted.

C H A P T E R   1 1

HOW PERSONALITY AFFECTS COMMUNICATION

When I look at the people at work, I see how God made them unique creations. There are so many variations of personalities. But the other day it dawned on me that yes, we're different, but there are also similarities. I guess we're different and similar at the same time.

Have you ever been frustrated with a coworker because he always seems preoccupied with "who knows what" that doesn't even pertain to the job at hand?

Do you ever start the day at work with great intentions to get a few specific things done but then get distracted?

Have you ever been excited about going to a church fellowship so that you can spend time with a lot of your friends? Or perhaps you don't care for these social events where you have to endure another evening of shallow conversation.

Does it ever surprise you when people view you as insensitive and uncaring at work when deep inside you are very sensitive and care deeply for others?

Have you ever left a business meeting confident that you've made a good impression only to have a colleague suggest there were at least 10 things you could have said better or shouldn't have said at all?

Do your coworkers seem to be calm and relaxed, with ample time to play, while you feel like a hamster on a treadmill?

STRANGE AND WONDERFUL DIFFERENCES

Nowhere is the breadth of God's creativity more evident than in humankind. No two of us are exactly alike. Even identical twins can have opposite personalities. Each of us has a combination of gifts, talents, attitudes, beliefs, needs and wants that is different from anyone else's. It's all right to be different! But is it all right for some of the people you work with to be *so* different? What accounts for these differences?

Why do some people love to be alone for hours on end and others go crazy if other people aren't around? Why is one coworker always coming up with new ideas and inventing things, while another is content to use things the way they are "supposed" to be used? (Which one of these two descriptions fits you best?) Why do some people like to talk things out while others prefer to work it out for themselves and then talk about it? Why does one person welcome a new employee and another act as if it's the end of the world? How can some people read a book for an hour without being bored or distracted, while others start climbing the wall after only 10 minutes? Why do some people take pride in having a clean and neat office, while other offices appear as if they've been used for nuclear testing?

In Psalm 139:14 (*TLB*) we read the words, "Thank you for making me so wonderfully complex! It is amazing to think about. Your workmanship is marvelous—and how well I know it." The Bible clearly teaches that every person is made in the image of God and is of infinite worth and value. That includes everyone where you work, as well as those you serve with at church.

After discussing in previous chapters the differences between men and women and

Nowhere is the breadth of God's creativity more evident than in humankind. Each of us has a combination of gifts, talents, attitudes, beliefs, needs and wants that is different from anyone else's.

their communication styles, you may be thinking, *But not all men are alike! Some men are so different from other men. Some women are quite different from other women, too. Why is that? And how do I figure out the best way to talk to someone who is so unlike me?*

Differences in personality type is the reason you see such variations among people.

UNDERSTANDING PERSONALITY TYPE

What is personality type? Where did it come from? How does it work? Personality type consists of several inborn preferences or tendencies that have a strong impact on how we develop as individuals. Every person begins life with a small number of inherited personality traits that make each person a little different from everyone else. Do you know what some of your traits are? What was it about you that made you a little bit (or a lot) different from your mom and dad, brother or sister?

Each trait is a fundamental building block of personality. These basic inborn traits determine many individual differences in personality. While core traits are present at birth, they are influenced and modified by our environment and how we are reared.

There are numerous personality theories and explanations. The one we are going to use is the *Myers-Briggs Type Indicator* (MBTI). The MBTI provides a practical way to identify, translate and understand core differences in personality. The MBTI identifies four sets of contrasting personality traits or *preferences*: extroversion and introversion (E or I), sensing and intuition (S or N), thinking and feeling (T or F), judging and perceiving (J or P). Each trait can be identified by its complete name or by the single letter assigned to it. A preference is the conscious or unconscious choice a person makes in a certain designated realm.

How People Gather Energy and Respond
Extroversion (E) _____ (I) Introversion

How People Gather Data and Information
Sensing (S)_____ (N) Intuition

How People Make Decisions—by Their Head or Heart
Thinking (T)_____ (F) Feeling

How People Structure Their Lives
Judging (J)_____ (P) Perceiving

According to type theory, everyone uses all eight of the traits, but one trait out of each of the four pairs is preferred and more fully developed. This concept is similar to the fact that while we have two hands and use both of them, we tend to prefer one hand over the other. Most people are either right-handed or left-handed. When using your most preferred hand, tasks are usually easier, take less time, are less frustrating and the end result is usually better.

As these various preferences are presented, you will find many variations. For example, one extrovert may fit all of the characteristics mentioned. In fact, on a scale of 0 to 10, this particular E may be a 10 and would be what we call a total E, whereas another extrovert may be a 6 on the scale. Some may find themselves having characteristics of both preferences in each pair. That's quite normal, since they may not have a strong preference either way.

The MBTI is a tool that doesn't stereotype people or place them in watertight boxes. It's more like a zip code. It tells you the state, city and neighborhood but not the specific address.

A key aspect of the MBTI is its nonjudgmental nature. The MBTI was grounded in the belief that while different approaches to interacting exist among individuals, no one given set of preferences is better or worse than any alternative set of preferences. Thus, the MBTI *does not* attempt to change behavior to meet a given ideal, but rather *encourages* individuals to understand and appreciate their own and others' personality preferences.

A person can be extreme and never access the nonpreferred trait. Then his or her strongest trait, which has not been balanced by the opposite trait, becomes a liability. As with drinking, eating, or certain other things, too much of a good thing can lead to trouble. If a person exercises any one preference too strongly or makes it too clearly defined, it may become more of a curse than a blessing.

EXTROVERSION AND INTROVERSION

The first set of preferences are called extroversion and introversion. Let's summarize what these traits are like.

I'm sure you have your own definitions of what extroversion and introversion mean, but it's important to be clear about them. These traits designate the way people prefer to interact with their environment. An extrovert (E) gains energy from being with people. There are a lot of them in this country—three extroverts for every introvert. An introvert (I) is energized by being alone and likes privacy.

Energy flows into extroverted types when they are around people. Energy flows into introverted types when they are able to reflect quietly.

The extroversion and introversion preferences focus on how you gain energy. We are like batteries. When a battery is attached to a charger, energy flows into the battery. When the battery is powering a lightbulb, energy flows out of the battery. Energy flows *into* extroverted types when they are around people. It's as though they suck it in. Energy flows *out* of, or drains, extroverted types when they are quietly reflecting on issues. That is why the E at work looks for others to talk with—even on the phone.

In contrast, energy flows *into* introverted types—charges them—when they are able to reflect quietly; energy flows *out* of them when they are interacting with others.

Characteristics of an Extrovert

E's (for extrovert, remember) are social creatures. "People energy" is what they feed on. They are approachable by friends and strangers alike. Sometimes they may tend to dominate a conversation. Invite them to a six-hour party and they're on cloud nine. At the end of the party they're wired and ready to go out with friends for coffee. They talk with everyone; in fact, they may share too much personal information too soon.

E's are not the best listeners. For them, listening is harder than talking because they have to give up the limelight. They may also have a tendency to interrupt as well as finish others' sentences.

E's have been described as walking mouths. Garrison Keillor, a popular monologuist and author said, "I talk until I think of something to say."[1] Instead of thinking first, E's talk first and really have no idea what they're going to say until they hear themselves talking. They brainstorm aloud for the entire world to hear and often need to think out loud to come up with the answer. The ideas they come up with aren't set in concrete; they're still being worked out, but E's let everyone else in on the process. E's tend to talk faster, louder and are a bit more animated than introverts (I's). E's also prefer a large playing field in life without too many boundaries.

E's typically like noise. They may want the radio or TV on at work, which can irritate others. They look forward to the interruptions of phone calls; if the phone doesn't ring, they will start calling people. When they come home, they will turn on the TV and/or stereo even though they don't watch or listen. They like noise in the background.

During a conflict they will talk louder and faster. They believe that if they can say just one more thing, everything will be fine. This can prolong group or committee meetings at church or the workplace.

E's feel lonely if other people aren't around much. You would think that E's are very secure based on the way they connect with people; but they have a high need for affirmation and compliments from everyone, especially from significant people.

If you have E's as employees or coworkers, you need to give an abundance of affirmations or they'll come looking for them. They may think they've done a good job, but they won't believe it until they hear it from someone else. They frequently will ask you for your opinion on various matters.

Characteristics of an Introvert

I's, on the other hand, need to formulate what they are going to say in the privacy of their minds before they're ready to share their thoughts and ideas. Ruth Ward, in her book *Blending Temperaments*, comments,

> Introverts generally engage in "mind-editing," which reduces verbal blunders but produces slower responses. "By the time I sift and decide what I want to say," one businessman introvert complained, "someone else has either verbalized what I intended to say or has moved on to another subject. Frustrating. I just listen."[2]

If pressured to give an immediate answer, their minds shut down. They usually respond with, "Let me think about that" or "I'll get back to you on that."

I's will participate far more in board or committee meetings when they are given the discussion questions or topics well in advance. Often their responses have a greater depth because of the thinking that preceded their comments.

Often I's are seen as shy or reserved. They prefer to share their time with one other person or a few close friends. They are usually quiet among strangers. They love privacy and need quiet time to themselves. They learn how to concentrate and shut out noise. On the other hand, I've seen many I's who are very gregarious and great conversationalists. They are socialized introverts. But at the end of the day they're exhausted and need quiet time to recharge.

Invite I's to a six-hour office party and they respond, "Six hours! You've got to be kidding. What will I do for six hours? I'd be wiped out!" So they go late, talk to selected people one at a time and leave early. That's what is comfortable for them. They may not care for the fellowship time in a class or a church service either.

I's are good listeners and hate to be interrupted when they talk. They may end up avoiding those who do interrupt them. When they're in a relationship they tend to keep their thoughts to themselves and wish their partner would too if he or she is an E.

I's tend to be cautious when entering a new relationship. They are slower to make friends in a new work setting. When asked a question, I's usually take an average of seven seconds before responding. (The problem is, if the other person is an E, that person usually waits about a second and a half before jumping in to give an answer or ask the question again).

Our schools are geared toward E children. The teacher asks a question and all the E children raise their hands. They don't know the answer yet; they will formulate it as they talk out loud. If the teacher would say to the class, "Here's a question I have for you. I'd like all of you to think about your answer for 20 seconds and then I'll tell you when to raise your hands," it would give equal opportunity to the I's.

I's wish other people would rehearse their thoughts as they do. They can carry on great internal conversations, including what the other person said. They can carry on a dialogue so realistically that they believe the conversation actually took place. This is where some misunderstandings occur at work.

I's are suspicious of compliments. In turn they may be sparing in giving them. Their E coworkers or employees end up wondering how they're doing. And since I's do not like being the center of attention, do not give them compliments in front of many people. Do it in private or, better yet, in writing.

Around work they are comfortable just being around others without a lot of activity and noise. I's are more comfortable with a "playing field" that is smaller. They want one they can control themselves. They have clearer boundaries and their motto is "You stay out of my territory and I'll stay out of yours."

E and I Compatibility

Can I's and E's work together without a lot of misunderstanding? What if they are extreme in their I or E preference? You might assume that an I would be more compatible with an I and an E with an E because of their similarities. But other aspects of our personalities need to be factored in because they play a part in the compatibility equation.

Frankly, any two personality combinations take work. It's all right for an E to be an E and an I to be an I. I've seen many people who get along well when they understand these differences and learn to adjust to one another. Those who have the same preference or who are closer together may find that working together comes more easily, but they will still need to work on bringing into play the strengths of the preference they lack.

What can two different preference types do to work together well? They can accept the differences and uniqueness of those around them and give others permission to be the way they are. They shouldn't try to make others like themselves. And they can praise God for the strengths in each preference, such as the E's ability to connect socially and the I's stability, strength and depth of thinking.

E's need to remember that I's can be exhausted by superficial socializing. I's will prefer less frequent get-togethers with just a few people, particularly those they are comfortable with. Don't pressure I's to always be with people. An E can help in a large gathering by *not* introducing a new I coworker to everyone, making them the center of attention. An E can also try not to talk too loud, call on an I to pray out loud in a large group or ask an I a question that requires an immediate response.

When an E has a question for an I, the best step an E can take is to say, "Here's something I'm interested in knowing. Why don't you think about it and let me know your response later." An I will appreciate this. In a gathering, an E could also single out and introduce individuals for the I with whom he or she would be comfortable in one-on-one conversations.

In a marriage or dating relationship, an E may want to ask her I partner to let her know when his battery has been drained and he needs to leave the party. In the same manner, an I needs to remember that an E partner thrives on being with people. I's could encourage their partners to get to a party ahead of them in order to have more time for socializing. Above all, an I needs to give an E partner more compliments than the I thinks is necessary!

One woman married into a family of eight (that's right, *eight!*) strong extroverts. At family get-togethers she can last for only about an hour. Then she takes a half-hour break by herself in another room to revitalize. You might think that's ridiculous or rude. No, it's reality and the only way it can work for her. We can't fight the way God created us as unique beings. Her in-laws now understand the differences between her preference and theirs, and they accept it.

When I's hear E's brainstorming out loud, they shouldn't assume that E's mean what they have just said. In a business setting, when an I manager hears several E's talking out loud about changes they'd like to see at work, the I will panic, since he wouldn't say anything unless he'd already thought it through. But the E's are just processing aloud for the whole world to hear. When this happens, just ask an E, "Are you brainstorming again?" and you'll probably hear a "Yes." On the other hand, it would be helpful for E's to announce what they're doing.

When I's are thinking about something, it would be helpful to let the other people around them know they are thinking and not ignoring the others. It's easy for an E to feel rejected when an

I doesn't say anything aloud (even though there's a lot of talking going on inside the I's mind).

CONFLICT SCENARIOS FOR E'S AND I'S

What are some problems that can occur in a business setting, or any setting, when extroverts and introverts interact?

An extrovert boss may tend to force introvert employees to engage in group discussions with limited time to think through their ideas.

What about the new work stations with their open-to-the-world configurations that afford little regard for privacy? Multiple conversations, excessive noise and no doors to bar invaders make it difficult for I's to concentrate and work effectively.

What about the E in sales who receives a promotion and now has an office with a closed door and has to deal with facts and figures on the computer rather than with people?[3]

Extroverts can monopolize meetings and cause introverts to shake their heads in confusion and frustration. For instance, it would not be unusual for the extrovert facilitator to walk into the meeting, present the problem, ask for opinions and give his own, come to his own conclusion, thank those present and leave without interrupting his own thinking process!

The introvert can cause a different kind of confusion. The I works inside his head, exploring alternatives and coming to a conclusion, but doesn't tell anyone, even though he thinks he did. The process inside his head was so real that he might think he shared it with everyone. And so disagreements arise.

The motto of the E is "Let it all out"; the I's motto is "Keep it in." This is why there are problems at work and in church settings between the different preferences.[4]

How do E's and I's approach goal-setting? The E's want to talk things through and make it a group experience. Unfortunately they believe that silence from the I's equals consent. And when the I's come back the next day with questions and suggestions, the E's are taken aback, saying, "I thought you were in agreement. You didn't say you were against this!"; to which the I replies, "But I didn't say I was for it either." I's would like to see information in writing to think about it for a while.

Both E's and I's need opportunity to deal with goals and decisions in their own way.[5]

So what about you? What is your preference for recharging your battery—are you an I or E? Do you need time alone or time with people? What about your coworkers? Remember, you can grow by understanding and adapting to these differences, so try to understand and accept them.[6]

Why not go back through the chapter now and write down each characteristic that describes you. (Yes, you may find some characteristics on both sides of the fence.) Then list how you will respond to others at work and at church in different ways than you have in the past, based on their preferences. You could be amazed at the results.

Notes

1. Ruth Ward, with John McRoberts and Marvin McRoberts, *Blending Temperaments* (Grand Rapids, MI: Baker Book House, 1988), p. 23.
2. Ibid., p. 21.
3. Otto Kroeger and Janet M. Thuesen, *Type Talk at Work* (New York: Delacorte Press, 1994), pp. 28, 29, adapted.
4. Ibid., p. 30, adapted.
5. Ibid., pp. 66-69, adapted.
6. Sandra Hirsh and Jean Kummerow, *Life Types* (New York: Warner Books, 1989), p. 16; Kroeger and Thuesen, *Type Talk at Work,* pp. 15, 16, adapted; David Luecke, *Prescription for Marriage* (Columbia, MD: The Relationship Institute, 1989), pp. 54, 55, adapted.

CHAPTER 12

HOW PEOPLE GATHER INFORMATION

I don't understand why others can't follow my directions. I know where I'm going and how to get there. Why can't they catch it? Some of them ask a million detailed questions. It's like we're talking two different languages!

The next set of preferences has a profound impact on communication in work relationships. These preferences reflect what sort of information you gather, how you gather it, the way you pay attention to it and the way you share it. You are either what the *MBTI Inventory* calls a sensor (S) or an intuitive (N).

A SENSOR'S LITERAL WORLD

If you are a sensor, you are keyed in to receive information through your five senses. What you pay attention to are the facts and details of situations. This is what you perceive, or notice, and it's what you believe.

What is it like to be an S? It shows up in your communication. When you ask a question, you want a specific answer (and that's the way you give answers). If you ask a coworker, "What time should I meet you?" and she says, "Around 4:00," that just won't do it. You may ask, "Does that mean 3:55, 4:00 or 4:05?" You are that literal.

I used to go fishing with a friend who was extreme in this regard. Anyone knows that when you ask your fishing partner if he has the bait over there, you're asking him to pass it to you. I mean, it's just obvious (at least to some of us). But when I'd ask Phil if he had the bait, he'd say, "Yes," and that was it. He wouldn't pass the bait over until I'd say, "Will you please pass the bait?"

If someone asks you if you have the time, you say, "Yes"—but you don't tell him the actual time until he asks. You don't assume; you force others to be specific.

If you're looking at something to purchase and a friend says, "It's a good deal; it's less than $100," that won't do either. You want the bottom line. (Remember, the stronger your preference in this area, the more precise you want things to be. If you're more toward the middle of the sensor scale, the less intense you are about getting precise facts).

As an S, you tend to be a focused person. You have a high level of concentration on what you're doing *now*—at the present moment. The future? Deal with it when it arrives. Don't waste time wondering what's next. Your motto is "One thing at a time." S's have little use for fantasy. They wonder why people assume, speculate and imagine. What good does it do?

You are a doer. If you have a choice between sitting around thinking about something and performing a task, there's no question as to what you'll do. You want to invest your efforts in tasks that yield results you can see.

Theories don't thrill you, but good old facts do. This probably affects the type and style of preaching or teaching you respond to. When you hear something from another person, you want it delivered sequentially—A to B to C to D. You don't like it when others meander off the path. It comes naturally for you to catalogue physical facts, dates, figures and details.

If you are a sensor, you receive information through your five senses—you pay attention to facts and details. If you are an intuitive, you look for the underlying meaning of relationships—for possibilities.

One of the S's biggest frustrations is when others do not give clear guidelines or instructions. After all, S's are very explicit and detailed when they tell someone something. So it really bothers them when they receive instructions that are just general guidelines.

For example, if you ask an N, "Where's the nearest Starbucks?" the N will say, "Go on down to 17th St. and turn left. It's a couple of blocks down on the right. You can't miss it." But an S would say, "Turn around and go back out the way you came in. Turn left and go a block and a half to 17th St. and turn left. It's three-and-a-half blocks down on the left, sandwiched between Kentucky Fried Chicken and a dry cleaners in a brick building."

S's have difficulty seeing the overall plan of something because they focus on what they are doing—they see the individual tree but not the forest.

When it comes to money, S's are very exacting. Money to them is tangible. When they have it they can use it, but only as much as the amount allows.[1] The S's view of money is that it's a tool to be used. That's it.

Predictability in a job gives them a sense of security, whereas change throws them. When it comes to the workplace or participation on church boards, both venues are involved in the attainment of goals. For an S to get excited and involved with a goal, it has to be one he can get his hands on and see results all along the way to the conclusion. A sensor wants goals to be simple and attainable. S's operate by the KISS (Keep it Simple Stupid) model of living, which they invented. A goal needs to be tangible rather than inspirational.[2]

The S's literalness is especially evident when it comes to time. Don't say to an S, "I'll be there in a minute," because she will expect you in 60 seconds. S's have a hard time understanding that for some people time is relative.[3]

Remember that I said every different type has a problem with procrastination? Well, it happens to S's as well. They procrastinate when they have to be involved in dreaming about the future and become a visionary in some way. They will find anything else to do, such as paying bills, doing a project that could wait, etc.[4] If you find an S coworker or fellow church board member procrastinating, take a look at what they're putting off, and that could tell you why.

Many sensors serve as bankers, doctors, nurses, mechanics, bookkeepers, administrators, secretaries, teachers, factory workers, salespeople and in many other product-related service careers.[5]

I was teaching an MBTI seminar to a company of 140 employees and made the comment that often you will find sensors in the accounting department. At that comment, I saw eight hands go up and heard several say, "Here we are." We all laughed at the obvious confirmation of what S's do well.

S's do have a preference for the routine. They are rule and direction followers. After all, isn't that what directions and rules are for? When an S talks to someone, the stories will be factual and accurate and make a lot of sense. This is what they need from others as well. When you are going to talk to an S, it might help the S if you list your points on paper in chronological order![6]

N's and the World of Possibilities

If your preference is intuitive, the way you respond to the world is *not* through the five senses or by facts but on the basis of your "sixth sense" or "hunches." Details and facts have their place (perhaps), but you can easily become bored with them. You don't take things at face value; instead, you look for the underlying meaning of relationships. You look for *possibilities*—a *very* important word for intuitives. Your focus is not on the here-and-now but on the future.

N's are sometimes perceived as a bit absentminded. Why? Simply because they like to think of several things at once. Sometimes it's difficult for them to concentrate on what's going on at the moment because the future has so many intriguing possibilities. N's live for the future. Today? Its purpose is to help get ready for tomorrow! If an N is going on a trip somewhere, the trip has already started weeks in advance. N's experience it during all the preparation time. For S's the trip doesn't begin until they have arrived at their destination; then they can begin to experience it.

There is another significant difference between S's and N's. When N's are describing something, it's as though they're actually experiencing what they're describing.

Jim (an N) was a new member on a subcommittee of a church board. The other three members were all S's. Jim had traveled to Mexico on several occasions. Since the church was only 150 miles from the border, he shared with the others all the possibilities of ministry for their youth group. He knew the board was looking for some way to challenge the senior high students in the area of missions.

He told the others it wouldn't cost much to take the youth group to Mexico since they could take tents and sleeping bags and stay in campgrounds along the way as well as at the mission where they would be working. He told about places and people and different cultures the kids would see and experience. The more he talked the more expressive he became. His description had almost come to life for him. By the time he finished talking, he was expecting the others to be just as enthusiastic as he was. It didn't happen.

They were anything but thrilled with the idea since, as S's, they saw all sorts of problems with Jim's idea. The questions rolled out one after the other. "We don't have a bus; who will drive?" "What if a car breaks down? There are problems with that in Mexico." "Is it really safe to camp?" "Where will the kids eat?" "What about showers?" "Who will go as chaperone?" "What about insurance?"

Jim was taken aback by their reticence. He was sharing with them a wonderful ministry opportunity. The problem was, he hadn't said it was a dream; he had presented it as though it would happen and they took everything he said literally. If Jim had presented the ministry opportunity in their language, giving them factual logistics, and had anticipated their questions by giving them detailed answers, they would have responded in a more positive manner. Jim thought he was talking to other intuitives. This misunderstanding happens all the time at church meetings and in work situations.

I was teaching on the S and N preferences in a class at church. Following the session, a man approached me and said, "I'm an N. I'm also an engineer. All the other engineers are S's. I've figured that out in this class. When I talk to them and share ideas, I usually get a puzzled look and the response, 'I don't understand a thing you just told me.' Now I'm beginning to understand why we've had this problem through the years."

N's have a unique way of dealing with time—to them it's relative. They may have a watch but it doesn't help them to be on time. "Late" doesn't register with them unless an event has started without them. They may also be late because they tried to do too much before they left. They thought they would be able to complete those five tasks before leaving for a meeting, but at the time they were supposed to leave they were halfway through the second project and wanted to complete it. Time clock jobs are very distracting to them. Can you see how this tendency can impact an office when others are dependent upon everyone's timely contribution?

OPPOSITE APPROACHES TO LIVING

Dr. David Stoop shares a choice example of the differences in the way an N and an S approach life:

> Intuitive people do things quickly. They start down the hill and soon find a ski jump. As they fly through the air, they land at the bottom of the hill. It took them less than a minute to get there, and they sit down and wait for their sensing spouses. When those people arrive, the intuitive people ask them, "What on earth took you so long?" After the sensing people relate all that they have seen on the way down the mountain, they stop and ask the intuitive people, "How did you get here?" Intuitive people can only say, "I don't know how, but I got here." Sensing people then reply, "It may take me longer, but at least I know how I got here." The sensing people see a lot of the details as well, whereas intuitive people are so

quick to jump to a conclusion, they miss the details and sometimes miss out on the joy of the moment.[7]

Instead of accepting things at face value, N's want to probe deeper, always asking, "Why is it this way?" They can drive an S crazy with their inquisitive, speculative nature and with their general and imprecise responses even to specific questions.

S's can get frustrated in committee meetings with N's because N's tend to see the forest rather than the individual trees, so specifics slip by them. They ask lots of questions and throw out endless possibilities, which needlessly prolong meetings, to a sensor's way of looking at things. On the other hand, even if the intuitives in the meeting are looking at the forest, they may not see it because their minds are elsewhere, and they may not even hear what has been said.

If an N and an S are watching a TV show, and the S comments about something just seen, the N might say, "Where was that?" It was right in front of the N, but something triggered a thought that sent the N's mind careening off the subject and she began speculating about something else entirely! This is common behavior for an N and can result in some misunderstandings when an S interprets it as not respecting what the S is saying or not being interested in the what the S and the N are doing together.

Differences in Handling Money

And then there are finances! Balancing the checkbook for an N is a chore. It's more intriguing to speculate how you're going to spend your next paycheck. Money creates opportunities, and who knows what doors it can open for you? N's see the value of money in terms of its possibilities. They are drawn to investment opportunities because they see the possibility of making a lot of money. They ignore the risk factor. What do you think would happen in your company if an N was the financial controller?

The way N's figure out how much money they have is intriguing. They're very adept at rounding off—either way up or way down! Some N's round *down* in their checking account any amount under 50 cents and round *up* any amount over 51 cents They have an exciting approach to money that may both intrigue and threaten an S.

Differences in Relationship Expectations

N's tend to view relationships optimistically—at times even unrealistically. The subtle indications that a relationship is progressing are important to an N—signs such as gifts, cards and remembering special dates. Change and variation in a relationship is very important. They believe that the roles and expectations of a relationship are negotiable and open to change.[8] What might this approach do for a long-term relationship between companies in the business world who are dependent upon one another?

About 70 percent of our population are sensors and 30 percent are intuitives. What if you work closely with someone who is in the opposite camp? How many sensors and how many intuitives do you think there are where you work? What about on your church board?

HOW S AND N DIFFERENCES ARE COMPLEMENTARY

S's are seen as rock-solid persons. N's are seen as creative, and their minds seem always to be in motion, figuring things out just for the fun of it. If an S were to draw a picture it would look similar to a Norman Rockwell. An N's picture would look similar to a Picasso.

To illustrate the differences between sensors and intuitives, a class was divided into two groups based upon whether they were S's or N's. Each group was placed in a separate room with cans of Tinker Toys. The only instructions were to make a building out of the Tinker Toys.

The building the sensors made was very precise and so strongly built that it could survive an 8.0 earthquake. But it was lacking style, beauty and creativity. To an intuitive it would be too functional and even boring.

The building the intuitives constructed was a work of art. It would enrich the decor of any room. But there was one problem. You could blow it over with one puff. There was no strength to the structure.

For the Tinker Toy building to have both beauty and strength, the S's and N's would have needed to work together.

What happens in a church board meeting or in a company if everyone is either an S or an N? There may be a type of one-sided strength, but there are certainly major weaknesses as well.

Can you begin to see now how an S and N might be intrigued by one another's differences? The staunch, steady one may admire the free-spirited butterfly. Can you also see the potential for driving each other up the wall with these same tendencies if each fails to realize they need the other's capabilities for balance?

ACCEPTING THE DIFFERENCES

Although an S would prefer an N to respond more like an S, and the N would prefer an S to be more like an N, it is critical that each learn to work with the differences. Don't wait for the other person to take the first step toward acceptance. Be a model. Learn to honor and respect the uniqueness of the person who is opposite to your information-gathering preference. To do this you will need to do two things: learn how to flex (and accomplish this to some degree), and also let the other person be who he or she is (realizing that this person is contributing something to you that you do not have). There are some things, however, to consider as you work toward acceptance and appreciation of the other person.

If you are an S, an N coworker will challenge you with possibilities you've never considered. That's healthy. You need that. Be willing to consider these possibilities instead of immediately responding in a negative manner. Accept the fact that what the N does or says will probably raise your anxiety over the risk factor. That's all right.

When N's sometimes fail to notice something you've done for them, like bringing coffee or doing a favor, let them know at an appropriate time that it's important to you for them to notice and comment. And if you're an N, make it a point to notice and comment! Write yourself reminder notes to respond to others at work with appreciation and a thank-you.

If you're an S, you're *not* responsible for an N's restlessness or discontent. You haven't caused it and you can't fix it. They experience more of the world than an S does.

TAILORING YOUR VERBAL RESPONSES

How can S's and N's work together so they can enjoy each other's differences? Although an N can be frustrated when an S isn't wildly enthusiastic about some of her dreams and ideas, an S may be enthused if the N presents the ideas simply and factually and suggests that her S employer or coworker think about it.

An S needs the facts in order to respond. Remember, an S will take care of the details that an N tends to overlook. And it's vital that the N express gratitude for this.[9]

An N needs to remember that what is said to an S will be taken at face value. In other words, it will be taken *literally*. So if you're an N, do a reality check when you talk. Don't assume that what you said was what the S heard or that what you meant was what he understood.

Let's consider some of the differences in the speech patterns of an S and an N. S's tend to use complete sentences when they speak, and they end these sentences with a period. It's definite. Emphatic. N's spin out sentences that omit certain information they assume the other person knows. They are tentative; they end sentences with a dash.

When these two types talk to one another, and they listen to the other according to their preferred trait, they can falsely assume the other person is talking their language. Big mistake!

Say that an S asks an N if he'd like to go to a pro football game on Sunday since he has an extra ticket, and the N says, "No . . . I don't think so—" The S assumes the N meant no with a period. Not so! It was a dash. So when Friday comes, the N may ask, "What time is the game on Sunday?" The S looks surprised and says, "What are you talking about? You said you didn't want to go!" The N replies, "I know I said that, but that's not what I meant. I needed to check on some things first and I got them cleared up to make sure I could make it!"

Overcoming this kind of difference requires an understanding of the intuitive's communication style. Dr. David Stoop describes the intuitive mind in terms of an iceberg. Ten percent is above the water where it can be seen; 90 percent is underwater. The part the N can't articulate won't pop to the surface for a couple of days or until someone helps the N articulate it. Stoop says,

> It's important to know that you will never find out what the dash of the intuitive person means by asking a question. If that is what you do, you will simply get a rehash of the information that has already been given. Instead, the sensing person must paraphrase back to the intuitive person what he or she heard the intuitive person

say, and then allow the intuitive person to add to what has been said already. And this paraphrasing needs to be repeated until the intuitive person says, "Yes, that's what I've been trying to say to you."

When intuitive people write out a first draft of a note or memo and then look at what they wrote, they will often add more information between the lines or up the side of the paper with an arrow to show where the thought goes. They do this because when they write they can see the part of the iceberg that is still underwater.[10]

It may help after a discussion for an S to ask an N, "Now, is that said with a period or a dash?" I've done this and it helps.

It's also helpful to understand how both the S and the N deliver information. When an S talks, he usually identifies the topic and moves through it factually and sequentially, although a bit unimaginatively for an N. But an N may start talking without identifying the subject, give three or four sentences of background material, go around the barn twice and *then* arrive at the subject. Can you imagine what the S is doing all this time? Probably climbing a wall.

Both the S and the N can learn to adjust to these opposing communication styles. When the N starts sharing but hasn't yet identified the topic, instead of getting frustrated an S can relax and realize he or she will get the background information first. When the subject is identified he will get the entire picture. It just won't be packaged the way the S would have done it—and that's all right.

When talking to an N, an S can learn to add more possibilities and details to his speech, which the N desires. It will help the S to become more flexible and take on some of the N's style. On the other hand, an N can work at identifying the subject in advance and letting the S partner know the topic. An N needs to practice being as factual and specific as possible.

By the way, have you ever heard two N's talking? Neither finishes a sentence but both know exactly what the other is talking about. It's amazing!

I'm an S and my wife, Joyce, is an N. (We can both access our nonpreference side as well. After 40 years of marriage, you do learn to do some things.) Every now and then Joyce will come to me and look me in the eye and say, "OK. Here's the bottom line, Norm" and she'll give me a two-line factual summary. We'll both laugh because on many occasions she will start by giving me three or four sentences of background material and then identify the topic. When she does this, I've simply learned to wait. I'm going to get the same information but in a different order. Similar to the German language sentence structure, the topic is at the end.

What happens when you begin putting the different preferences together? What do you think an ES is like compared to an EN? Or an ES working with an IN? Why not take some time right now and outline or list the various possibilities of these combinations. (Did you catch the wording choices I used that would appeal to both an S and an N)?

Remember, you need the differences of the opposite preference in your life. Yes, it may be uncomfortable at times, but we all need to be stretched in order to grow. When we flex to understand, accept, and even use our nonpreferred trait, we will all get along better.

Notes

1. Otto Kroeger and Janet M. Thuesen, *Type Talk* (New York: Bantam Books, 1988), pp. 17, 18, adapted.
2. Otto Kroeger and Janet M. Thuesen, *Type Talk at Work* (New York: Delacorte Press, 1992), p. 20, adapted.
3. Ibid., p. 99, adapted.
4. Ibid., p. 99, adapted.
5. Ruth McRoberts Ward, *Blending Temperaments* (Grand Rapids, MI: Baker Book House, 1988), p. 26, adapted.

6. Ibid., p. 53, adapted.

7. Dr. David Stoop and Jan Stoop, *The Intimacy Factor* (Nashville, TN: Thomas Nelson Books, 1993), pp. 72, 73, adapted.

8. Sandra Hirsch and Jean Kummerow, *Life Types* (New York: Warner Books, 1989), pp. 30, 31, adapted.

9. David L. Luecke, *Prescription for Marriage* (Columbia, MD: The Relationship Institute, 1989), pp. 58-60, adapted.

10. Stoop and Stoop, *The Intimacy Factor,* pp. 80, 81.

CHAPTER 13

HOW PEOPLE
MAKE DECISIONS
AND STRUCTURE
THEIR LIVES

*Some of the people on our church board seem to make their decisions based on
something other than reasoning. To me they're kind of wishy-washy. Why can't
they think it through better and use their minds? You know . . . like me.*

Do you struggle over making decisions? Do you wonder why
others at work make decisions differently from the way you do?
Do you wonder how a person came to the decision he made? Do
you wonder why some people seem to have no problem with
making quick decisions? All of these questions can be answered
by understanding your preference in using either a thinking process or a feeling process when you make decisions.

Some people are thinkers (T); they make decisions quickly. Other people are feelers (F) who seem to take forever to reach a decision. Some people have a very sharp, clear, definite and decisive style, while others are cautious, gentle, investigative and option-oriented.

For a working relationship to succeed you will need to mesh your differences and develop your own decision-making style as a team or committee whether in a church setting or on the job. This third set of MBTI preferences—thinking (T) or feeling (F)—shows how you and others individually prefer to make decisions. These differences will definitely show up in the communication process.

Dr. David Stoop describes these two personality types:

Thinking people can stand back and look at the situation. They make a decision from an objective viewpoint, interpreting the situation from the outside. They believe that if they gather enough data they can arrive at the truth. They are always searching for this truth, which they believe exists as an absolute. These people see things as black-and-white, as absolutes. If the answer seems to lie in the gray area, thinking people believe they just haven't gathered enough data. If they can just look further, they will discover the truth.

On the other hand, feeling people always make decisions from a personal standpoint by

The thinking or feeling preference is the trait that reflects how you handle your emotions, even though the trait really has very little to do with your emotions themselves.

putting themselves into the situation. They are subjective, believing that two truths can exist side-by-side.

The difference between a thinking person and a feeling person can be seen in the way the two make decisions, such as buying a car. Thinking people get the consumer reports and do research into different types of cars. They ask themselves, "Which is the best financial value? Which is safest?" They'll decide which criteria is most important to them and then make a decision based on that criteria. When they go to the car dealership, they'll know exactly what they want, and even that persuasive car salesman can't talk them into buying another car.

Feeling people start looking at all the cars on the road. "Which car would I like to be driving right now?" they ask themselves. "What color looks good? What make? What style?" When feeling people arrive at the car dealership they may think, "I want a blue Honda coupe." But after they've looked around a while, they may fall in love with a metallic green Honda Accord. And that's the car they'll purchase—even if it costs more money.

The important questions to ask yourself are: How do I make a decision? Do I listen more to my head when I make good decisions, or do I listen more to my heart?[1]

So, what about you? When you make decisions, do you listen more to your head or to your heart? What about your coworkers? Have you even thought about this issue and how it affects your communication with them?

The thinking or feeling preference is the trait that reflects how you *handle* your emotions, even though the trait really has very little to do with your emotions themselves. A T is often uncomfortable talking about feelings. He or she may also be uncomfortable in the area of aesthetics and building relationships. Other people may see them as aloof and cool, even though they are actually quite sensitive.

F's are comfortable with emotions. Not only are they aware of their own feelings, they can sense what others are experiencing as well. When it comes to making a decision, they aren't just concerned with how it affects them but also how it affects others. This is why it may take them longer to make a decision.

If a T were on a jury, he would be concerned with justice and fairness. He would look at the facts, find the truth and make a decision. An F would be concerned with mercy. Facts are all right, but what are the circumstances in the case? Why did the person do what he did? An F would want to give the benefit of the doubt.[2] Who would you want to be on your jury?

Do you have an idea yet where you stand on this issue of thinking and feeling? How does your style impact your communication with others?

THE THINKER

If you are a T, you're the one who stays calm and collected in a situation when everyone else is upset. You keep your wits about you. You're the epitome of fairness when you make a decision. But you're not that concerned with what will make others happy. You're more firm-minded than gentle-minded. You want to make sure others know where you stand, whether they like it or not. You'll state your beliefs rather than have others think they are right. It's more important to have the office work smoothly than to have everyone like one another.

In fact, you're not concerned with whether people like you or not. What's important is being right. Your skin is quite thick. You can take it.[3] And argue? Sure—sometimes just for the fun of it. It's important for you to be objective even if others misinterpret you or your motives (if you're also an E, how might this affect arguments? Remember, an E believes one more statement would clear it up!).

If you're a T, you enjoy making hard decisions and you can't understand why it's so difficult for others. Anything logical or scientific impresses you. You're drawn to it. (If you're also an S, can you see what your communication style would be like?)

In your interpersonal relationships you may have difficulty remembering names. In a relationship you need logical reasons for the purpose of the relationship's existence. The way you look at others is not only very realistic, but it is also critical. You tend to correct and try to redefine other people. You may express this both verbally and nonverbally.

T's are reserved in the way they show love, and sometimes they show it quite impersonally. They don't want to be out of control. T's also have a built-in filter to screen out the emotional parts of communication. It's uncomfortable for them to share their emotions. The simple but important niceties in a relationship are lacking.[4]

THE FEELER

If you are an F you're the person with an antenna sticking out that picks up how others are feeling. And sometimes you allow them to dictate how you respond. You tend to overextend yourself to meet the needs of others, sometimes even if it costs you.

In coming to a decision you are always asking, "How will this affect other people?" Sometimes you end up with a sense of tension—you like to help others, but sometimes you feel that you're always giving while others are taking. You may feel that others take advantage of you and that your own needs aren't being met.

If you're an F, you are well liked. Why? Because you're the peacemaker for everyone. "Let's all get along" is your motto. Sometimes others wonder if you have much of a backbone. You tend to change what you've said if you think it has offended someone.

You're very aware of your own personal reasons for relationship. You see the best in others. You show your caring in a very personal way through words, cards, actions, etc. You're constantly scanning the other's messages to see if there's any emotional meaning to the words. Any offering of emotional response is appreciated unless it is negative. You don't want anything to undermine any kind of relationship.

This is the only preference in which there is a gender distinction. Sixty percent of men are T's and 40 percent are F's. Sixty percent of women are F's and 40 percent are T's.

One writer described the differences between a thinker and feeler in the following example. He was attending a conference. During a break, the baby of one of the participants somehow became locked inside a closet.

The thinkers in the group responded to the problem in a task-oriented way, unaware of the emotional needs of the distraught baby's mother. Their idea was "We have a problem—a baby locked in a closet. Let's find a way to liberate the baby."

The feelers responded to the mother's emotional upset and tried to reassure her. They were doing what they did best—responding to a hurting person. They seemed so concerned for the mother that it was as though they had forgotten someone needed to get the baby out of the closet.[5]

It's not uncommon for thinking people to intimidate feelers since they can give reasons for their decisions. Feelers know what they believe to be right but usually say, "I just know this is right inside" rather than list reasons. Some T's are so into reasons that they won't consider something new unless the other person can give at least three reasons for it.

Marriage Between a T and an F

One of the most typical relationships that develops is a T-male and F-female. This connection has the most potential for creating divisiveness and long-term problems. T's need to think about and analyze their emotions. They bring to a marriage emotional control and reserve that can limit intimacy. They want to *understand* intimacy, not experience it, while an F wants to share openly and *experience* intimacy.

If a couple doesn't learn to connect emotionally, they're at risk for either an affair or a marriage breakup. The bonding material of a marriage is emotional intimacy. F's hunger for warmth, sharing and closeness, and without this dimension they can end up feeling lonely. They like the inner strength and security of a T, but not the perceived emptiness.

Unfair as it sounds, a T will need to work more to adapt than will an F. Learning a vocabulary of intimacy and how to describe emotions is essential. A T's uniqueness is definitely needed, but it can also create a sterile relationship. T's and F's are attracted by each other's differences but at the same time are a bit repelled by them. A T desires intimacy but might fear it even more.[6]

Feelers need to work on being less subjective and feeling less responsible for everyone's emotional state. They need to take things less personally, to learn to become assertive and to face disagreements. They need to stop saying, "I'm sorry" and "It's my fault" so much.

A T and an F at Work

Can a T and an F work well together? Yes, but it will take constant work. You must avoid judging the other for the way he is and realize he will never become just like you. You can defeat yourself and put tension in the workplace by trying to make others think like you. Sure a T wants an F to be more analytical and efficient and to get to the point quicker. The F wants from the T more transparency, emotional expression and social awareness. To a point, both of you can learn to accommodate these concerns.

A T takes care of things and an F takes care of people. Do you see T's and F's where you work?

A T takes care of organization and an F provides warmth and harmony to the workplace. One without the other creates an imbalance. A T brings emotional control, while an F provides emotional energy.

A T gives structure; an F nurtures.

If you're a T, stretch yourself to enter into the social life provided by F's. Watch and listen to how F's interact. When you're talking to an F, be more expressive and tentative and use feeling words. You'll gain more friends that way. Accept the way F's share. Praise your partner for her feelings and tell her you need to learn what she has to offer.

If you're an F, remind yourself of the qualities of T's. Note how you make use of a T's characteristics. You'll need their problem-solving abilities. T's will add energy, organization and direction to your spontaneity. When you talk with a T, follow these guidelines:

Explain yourself clearly, logically and concisely. Thinkers often want to know the *why*. Give them the reasons before they ask for them.

Define your terms. For an F, some statements don't need any definition. For a T, the same simple statement can mean a number of things.

Listen for what T's say before attempting to interpret how they said it.

If you're a T, here's what you can do when you're talking to an F:

Provide plenty of verbal affirmation. Most F's thrive on praise and encouragement.

Remember that the language of an F is in some ways different from the language of a T.

Don't underestimate the value of "small talk." To most F's there is no such thing as small talk. When they share their weekend experiences at the office on Monday they aren't just downloading a list of data. They are giving you a part of themselves.

Don't listen to how logical their reasons are for what they are saying, listen for what they are feeling. Ask questions that draw them out.

A T simply will not respond in the same way socially or relationally as an F will. Don't interpret a T's cool reserve as personal rejection but as a personality trait. A comment that hurts probably wasn't intended to hurt you. You may need to positively guide a T in new ways to express things to you.[7]

Remember that you are a mixture of thinking and feeling preferences. One trait is dominant in you, so you may need to work on nurturing (I used a feeling word because I'm an F) your less dominant preference.

HOW WE APPROACH DAILY LIFE

Let's consider the last set of preferences—judging (J) and perceiving (P)—in light of a scenario that expresses each viewpoint. These traits represent how we are likely to respond to any life situation.

You are out to dinner at a restaurant and there's a couple sitting next to you. The waiter comes up to take the order and the wife says, "I'll have the ribeye cut, medium rare, baked potato with butter only and the salad with dressing on the side." The waiter asks, "What kind of dressing? We have French, bleu cheese, honey mustard, Italian and ranch." She replies, "Ranch."

The waiter turns to the man and he starts by asking several questions. He wants to know the difference between several of the steaks and which is the most popular. (By the way, this couple eats here regularly.) He looks around at several tables to see what others are eating. After all this he seems to have enough information to select a meal. He orders fish. Then he asks what salad dressings are available (even though the waiter already listed them for the wife). Just as the waiter starts to walk away, the man changes his mind and orders a steak.

Have you been around people like either the man or the woman? With which person do you identify?

The man and the woman's style of ordering dinner is a glimpse into how they approach all of life. In other words, some people approach life in a structured and organized manner, and some approach life in a free-flowing, spontaneous and adaptive manner. In the *MBTI Inventory*, people whose preference is structure are called judgers, while free-form types are called perceivers.

These preferences largely determine what you share when you begin to talk and are critical to the communication process. Let's consider these preferences in the realm of work.

The Judger

If you are a J, you are very conscious of time and schedules. It's as though you have a built-in clock. You seem to spend a good portion of your life waiting for others who don't have a clear understanding of time. If work begins at 8:30, you expect everyone to be there at 8:30. This can be a big source of irritation to you, especially if you're an SJ. Free time occurs only after you've set your schedule. Then you know what's left.

You're a list-keeper. You probably carry a list around with you. You're probably one of those persons who has a Day-Timer calendar system and who makes it work. Crossing off listed items gives you great satisfaction. Your entire day is mapped out from the time you wake up until bedtime. If something interferes with your schedule, watch out.

In school you probably completed assigned projects in advance. And you like order, from the way things are arranged in the cupboards to the color-coded clothes hanging a half inch apart in the closet, to the neatly arranged pens and pencils on your desk. Your motto is, "Get the work done first, then play." If you have a task to do, you'll keep at it until it's done, even if waiting would give you better resources to do a better job. It's irritating to see others at the office just sitting around socializing.

J's view interruptions and surprises as totally unnecessary. People around them soon learn to tell them about a change that's coming; then leave and let the J fuss for 10 minutes and get it out of his system; then come back and discuss it. If several changes in one day hit a J boss, the employees learn to keep their distance for a while. And it's helpful to give J's information in advance so they can think about it for a while. This is very important if a J is also an introvert.

In order to be spontaneous, a J has to plan it in advance! "A week from Sunday, I will be spontaneous from 1:00 to 5:00 P.M."

A J economizes on words and gives decisions but doesn't always provide enough data to back it up. (What might you be like if you are a J as well as an S (sensor) and a T (thinker)?) It's important to begin to notice the grouping of these traits and what they mean. At the conclusion of this chapter there are recommended resources if you want to learn more about the significance of each four-letter grouping.

J's think of money as something that provides security and one of the ways to measure their success and progress. The best thing to do with money? Simple—save it. This means investing wisely, budgeting, being careful in giving money away, prioritizing how to spend it and using it for your child's college and your retirement.

The Perceiver

Talk about opposites! The P loves adventure—the unknown is there to be explored, even if we're only talking about finding alternative routes home each day. Planning is not for you. It's too limiting. You would rather wait and see what unfolds.

If you are a perceiver, those who see you as disorganized just don't understand you. Neatness has little appeal for you. Sure, you would like to be organized, but that's not nearly as important as being *creative, spontaneous* and *responsive.* A pile of papers to a J is nothing more than a mess to clean up. But to a P, that pile of papers is like compost. If you leave it there long enough, something good is bound to happen! A J employer comes into a P's office and wonders how anything can be accomplished there.

What is time to a P? Even if you have a watch you don't look at it or want to be limited by it. You wait until the last minute to get things done and although you usually get them done, you upset others in the process. In school you probably pulled an all-nighter to get that paper done or prepare for an exam. And when this happens at work or with a church project, the J's get a bit anxious. Free time for a P is all the time except for what has to be scheduled.

As a P, your attention span is very flexible. That's another way to say you're easily distracted. Things have to be "fun." If someone tells you a work project will be fun, you respond positively. Just as the word "possibility" is so important to the N, "fun" is critical to the P. (These are good words for S's and J's to use in talking with their opposites.)

If you are a P, it's difficult for you to make up your mind or to decide on something. If you do, it may keep you from doing something better that might come along. You like options. So others see you as noncommittal, hesitant or not having the ability to make up your mind.

You may come home with clothes from the store but take them back the next day because you'll find something better at another store. Being definite is not your forte. You don't want to rule out anything by deciding one way or the other.

A P's motto is, "I'll get around to it" or "It's around here somewhere." (The word "ramble" comes to mind when describing a P). You can jump from one subject to another and the impetus for the change in topic may be something you saw through the window or on a TV show you just watched.

You are agile and flexible in your style of conversation. You don't need to resolve your discussions, even though you may go around the barn three or four times. When you make a point you may say it several different ways—it's as though you get paid by the word. But sometimes you're so vague that it's hard to follow your train of thought. If you're also an extrovert, everyone will hear you change your thoughts in the middle of a sentence and even interrupt yourself. And if you're an N . . . ! Think of all the possibilities! What fun! (J's and P's have some of the worst difficulties in communicating.)

It's an amazing experience for others to hear a P talking with another P because the conversation can go anywhere and in all directions at one time. You may not finish your sentences before moving on, but the other P follows you. (A J probably wouldn't be able to.) And if a person is an NP, what might his or her communication style be like?

Then there's the way you look at finances. Money is a means to help you get the most out of life. The best way to use it is to *spend it!* Ask P's what to do with money and you hear responses like "Have fun with it," "Enjoy it when you have it," "If you see someone in need, give them some," "Take a trip on the spur of the moment" or "Take some friends on a cruise."[8] (Major work conflicts occur over this attitude.)

Perceivers experience some tension when considering commitment. They're more hesitant because they don't want to cut off other options. Sometimes they are up and down over the status of their relationships. When they do commit, it's still open for reevaluation.

Whereas a J wants security, a P wants freedom. This tendency is also evident with the calendar. A J wants to keep the appointment come what may, while a P says, "I may go and then again something else may come up that interests me more."

If there's work to do on some issue, P's typically want to wait and deal with it when an issue arises. They'll look for ways to combine work and play. P's prefer to be creative, let it flow and see what develops.[9]

Often you hear a J saying to a P, "The problem with you P's is that you answer a question with another question." And the Perceiver responds with, "So . . . is that bad?"

HOW OPPOSITES APPROACH GOALS IN THE WORKPLACE

How do an F and a T approach goals at work? Well, a thinker creates a goal only after an exhaustive thought process. If it is the best goal possible and is useful and measurable, a T can be committed to it but doesn't have to agree with it or with the opinions of the coworkers.

For the F, a goal must reflect a concern for every person involved. A goal should be approved of by everyone and be beneficial for everyone. Will it help people live better or is it only for the bottom line?[10]

An example of the differences in thinking and feeling in decision making occurred in the Ford Motor Company in 1958. The thinking-oriented engineering company designed a new state-of-the-art car that had a radical new style and was technically advanced. They said this is what people wanted. But they didn't consult any feelers to find out how people would feel about the radical changes. Would people like it? Feelings were not taken into account.

People didn't like it. It didn't appeal. It wasn't attractive. Objective engineering couldn't overcome what people liked. The name of this car? The Edsel. I remember my own response when it came on the scene. Believe me, it was ugly.

Both objective facts and feelings need to be considered when you're dealing with the consumer.[11]

If you are a J or a P trying to connect with your opposite in the workplace, consider the strength each of you brings to the situation. A P is the one who expands information and alternatives before decisions are made. Some of these alternatives could be better than what the J has considered. The J will see that conclusions are reached and the decisions followed. You need each other for complete success.

Each of you will need to give more time in order to hear what the other has to say. Don't immediately think the other is wrong or try to convince him that you are right. Do not engage in name-calling. (P's tend to call J's close-minded, opinionated and stubborn; whereas J's are tempted to label P's as flaky, unsupportive or wishy-washy).

And above all, do not compete!

How the Differences Can Work Together

J's can encourage P's to take more time, consider alternatives and change their minds. It helps to use the word "fun" when talking to a P about changes. J's can also work on being less definite and emphatic when they make statements. They can give in to the other person and instead of always giving advice or conclusions, ask a question or two.

J's can give the P more responsibility for planning and decisions. Don't expect P's to immediately back your decisions. They need time to explore. Don't back the P into a corner by predetermining responses and solutions. J's must stretch their ability to live with unanswered questions, things appearing to be out of control and indecision.

If you are a J, remember that there is more than one right answer. Don't take a P's apparent lack of commitment and support personally. A P has a different timetable and intensity. Remember the P's motto: "I'll get around to it." Even that statement will be voiced tentatively.

Both of you, J and P alike, should purposefully do things the way the other does every now and then. In doing this at work you might be amazed at discovering new ways to complete tasks. And some styles of approaching work could be better than what you're doing now. Appropriating your nonpreferred trait now and then will help you to flex. And you may be surprised that you can do it.[12]

Thank each other for the way that you are. You need what the other has to offer. You may just be threatened by the differences.

If you're a P, above all make every effort to be on time when you have told a J you would be there. We live in a society that values punctuality. You could write yourself some reminder notes and place them where you can see them easily and frequently. Some jobs tolerate lateness; others don't.

Sometimes P's think they can get "just these four tasks completed" before they leave the office, and that contributes to their being late. The way to overcome this is to come up with the four things you think you can do; then just do one or two of them. You could probably finish these, feel good about it and still be on time. Perhaps you need to begin seeing yourself as a person who *is* on time!

As a P, be more definite when you share how you feel about some issues. Let the J's know that you're not challenging their decisions. You just need time to explore on your own. Keep in mind that what a J is saying may not be set in concrete, even if he says it is. Ask how important a decision is on a scale of 0 to 10; if it's anything more than a 6, follow through on it.

If you tend to drift off the topic in a conversation and the J brings you back to the issue at hand, thank him for doing so. You probably needed that.[13]

Remember that a J's needs for certainty and structure is who he is and not a personal vendetta to control you.

Some people believe they have an ideal work situation because everyone has the same set of preferences on the *Myers-Briggs Type Inventory*. Perhaps, but maybe not. The combination of your preferences does affect your work style, but both the preferences you have and the ones you do not have help determine the quality of how people get along.

You may have a complementary advantage when you have the same preference with a coworker but lack the advantage of the one you're missing. For example, if everyone at work is missing a certain preference, you would probably avoid the activities or experiences enjoyed by someone with that preference. You would have to make an effort to access your nonpreference side and learn to use it.

Remember that you do not, will not and cannot change another's personality type. You learn to adjust. No personality type is wrong. Your personality is God's gift to you. But perhaps the bridge between the different preferences may need to be relocated a bit so there can be a better traffic flow.

MULTIPLE SOLUTIONS FOR A SINGLE PROBLEM

Finally, let's consider how some T and J combinations might deal with a problem at work. The authors of *Type Talk at Work* describe this situation: A company calls to inform your company that the order you sent a week ago hasn't arrived. It's now 3:00 P.M. on Friday. They *must* have the order on Monday *or else*. How would different type combinations try to solve this problem?

ST's would probably accept the fact the order is lost and not waste time looking for it. Everyone would need to stay late, put together a new order and get it shipped ASAP. (Who on your church board or at work would fit this description)?

SF's would also accept the same fact but would poll the company to see who could work late. If no one else could do it, they'd do it themselves. (Who on your church board or at work would fit this description)?

NF's would consider the possibility that the order could be found, organize a search with one group and develop a second group to develop a Plan B. They would work to motivate both groups while doing the lion's share of the work themselves to make it easier for others. (Who on your church board or at work would fit this description)?

NT's would try to track down the order but also begin redoing the order just in case. They'd also work on putting together a third order just in case. They'd probably look into why something like this occurred, to make sure it didn't happen again.[14]

If you are interested in reading more about your personality type and the significance of how preferences are grouped, here are some resources to help you learn more:

Type Talk by Otto Kroeger and Janet M. Thuesen

Type Talk at Work by Otto Kroeger and Janet M. Thuesen

Why Can't I Be Me? by Mark A. Pearson

It *is* possible to get along better with others. It's not always easy, and yes, it will take some work on your part; but the good news is that you can make the changes that will allow you to enjoy your interactions with coworkers and anyone with whom you work for a common goal. The adaptation is well worth it!

Notes

1. Dr. David Stoop and Jan Stoop, *The Intimacy Factor* (Nashville, TN: Thomas Nelson Publishers, 1993), pp. 88, 89.
2. Ibid., pp. 90, 91, adapted.

3. Otto Kroeger and Janet M. Thuesen, *Type Talk* (New York: Bantam Books, 1988), pp. 18, 19, adapted.

4. David L. Luecke, *Prescription for Marriage* (Columbia, MD: The Relationship Institute, 1989), pp. 44, 45, adapted.

5. Mark A Pearson, *Why Can't I Be Me?* (Grand Rapids, MI: Chosen Books, 1992), p. 42, adapted.

6. Luecke, *Prescription for Marriage*, p. 43, adapted.

7. Ibid., pp. 64-69, adapted.

8. Kroeger and Thuesen, *Type Talk*, pp. 18, 19, adapted.

9. Ibid., pp. 21, 22, adapted. Otto Kroeger and Janet M. Thuesen, *16 Ways to Love Your Lover* (New York: Delacorte Press, 1994), pp. 86, 87, adapted.

10. Otto Kroeger and Janet M. Thuesen, *Type Talk at Work* (New York: Delacorte Press, 1992), pp. 74, 75, adapted.

11. Kroeger and Thuesen, *Type Talk at Work*, pp. 73, 74, adapted.

12. Luecke, *Prescription for Marriage*, pp. 71, 72, adapted.

13. Kroeger and Thuesen, *16 Ways To Love Your Lover*, p. 97, adapted.

14. Kroeger and Thuesen, *Type Talk at Work*, pp. 165, 166, adapted.

If You Liked the Book, You'll Love the Videos!

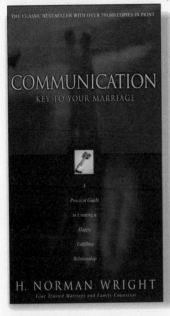

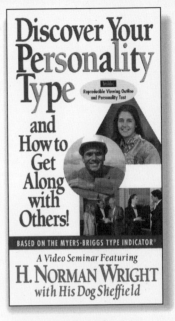

Communication: Key to Your Marriage
How to Create a Happy, Fulfilling Relationship
Video • Approx. 120 minutes
UPC 607135.004639

Discover Your Personality Type
How to Avoid Conflict by
Understanding Yourself and Others
Video • Approx. 140 minutes
ISBN 85116.01090

You couldn't put down his book. Now you can share H. Norman Wright's warmth and wisdom with a small group, your entire congregation or just enjoy it with your family at home! These videos featuring one of America's best-known Christian counselors prove a point: At last, there really is something worth watching on TV!

Unique Advantages of Video Training:

- Easily followed by any size group

- Ideal for people who don't like to read

- No need for an experienced speaker
  Lead a group study with video

Family Counseling & Enrichment Center
P.O. Box 2468, Orange, CA 92859-0468
1-800-875-7560